Rosemary Hawley Jarman

Crispin's Day
The Glory of Agincourt

COLLINS
14 St James's Place, London
1979

William Collins Sons & Co Ltd
London · Glasgow · Sydney · Auckland
Toronto · Johannesburg

First published 1979
© Rosemary Hawley Jarman, 1979
ISBN 0 00 216123/0
Set in Bembo 270
Made and Printed in Great Britain by
W. S. Cowell Ltd, Ipswich

REVERSE OF FRONTISPIECE: *Henry V's great seal*

Contents

For Linda Adams

Colour Plates

Acknowledgements

DESIGNER: Patrick Yapp

PICTURE RESEARCHER: Joy Law

CARTOGRAPHER: Tom Stalker Miller

INDEXER: Lysbeth Merrifield

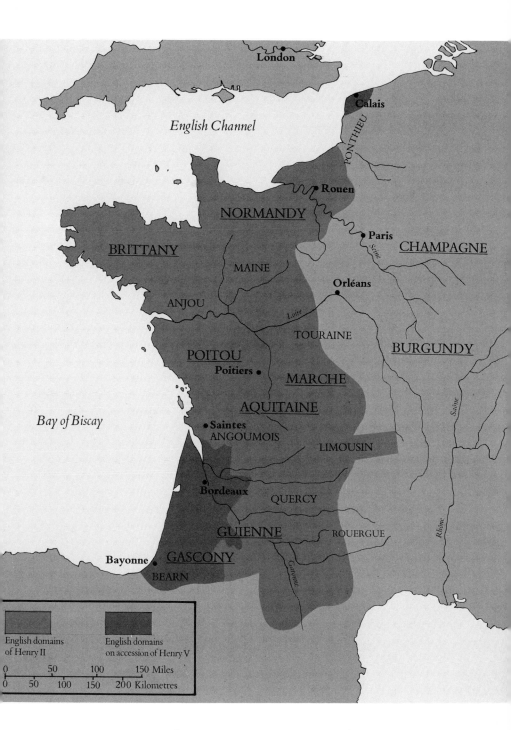

London

Calais

English Channel

PONTHIEU

Rouen

NORMANDY

Paris

CHAMPAGNE

BRITTANY

MAINE

Seine

ANJOU

Orléans

Loire

TOURAINE

BURGUNDY

POITOU

Poitiers

MARCHE

Saône

AQUITAINE

Bay of Biscay

Saintes
ANGOUMOIS

LIMOUSIN

Bordeaux

QUERCY

Rhône

GUIENNE

ROUERGUE

Bayonne

GASCONY

BEARN

Garonne

English domains
of Henry II

English domains
on accession of Henry V

| 0 | 50 | 100 | 150 Miles |
| 0 | 50 | 100 | 150 | 200 Kilometres |

The English possessions in France.

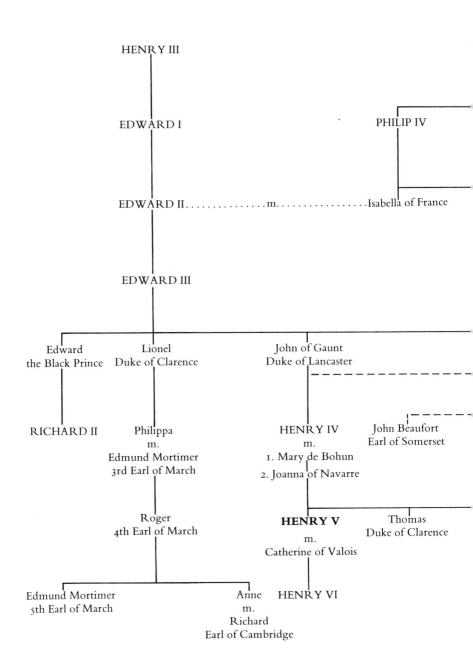

HENRY III

EDWARD I   PHILIP IV

EDWARD II . . . . .m. . . . . .Isabella of France

EDWARD III

| Edward
the Black Prince | Lionel
Duke of Clarence | John of Gaunt
Duke of Lancaster | |

| RICHARD II | Philippa
m.
Edmund Mortimer
3rd Earl of March | HENRY IV
m.
1. Mary de Bohun
2. Joanna of Navarre | John Beaufort
Earl of Somerset |

Roger
4th Earl of March

HENRY V
m.
Catherine of Valois

Thomas
Duke of Clarence

Edmund Mortimer
5th Earl of March

Anne   HENRY VI
m.
Richard
Earl of Cambridge

HENRY V's CLAIM TO THE FRENCH CROWN

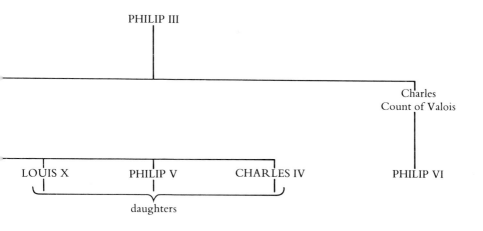

PHILIP III

Charles
Count of Valois

LOUIS X   PHILIP V   CHARLES IV   PHILIP VI

daughters

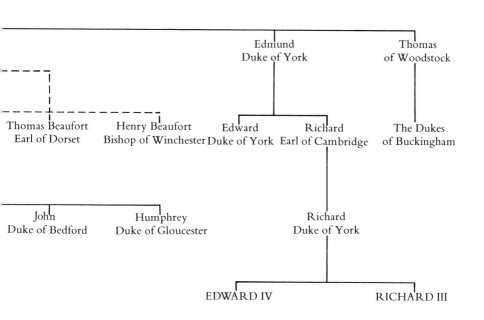

Edmund
Duke of York

Thomas
of Woodstock

Thomas Beaufort   Henry Beaufort   Edward   Richard   The Dukes
Earl of Dorset   Bishop of Winchester Duke of York   Earl of Cambridge   of Buckingham

John   Humphrey   Richard
Duke of Bedford   Duke of Gloucester   Duke of York

EDWARD IV   RICHARD III

CAPETIAN

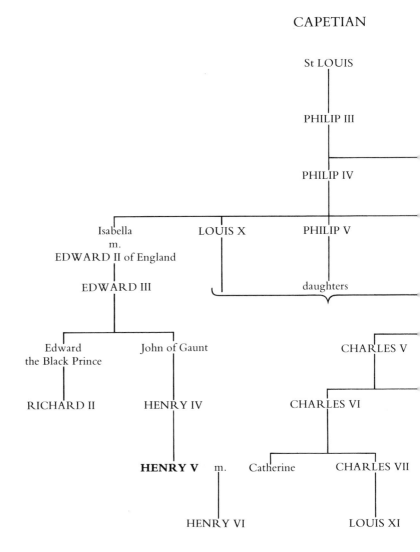

St LOUIS

PHILIP III

PHILIP IV

Isabella   LOUIS X   PHILIP V
m.
EDWARD II of England

EDWARD III   daughters

Edward   John of Gaunt   CHARLES V
the Black Prince

RICHARD II   HENRY IV   CHARLES VI

HENRY V   m.   Catherine   CHARLES VII

HENRY VI   LOUIS XI

THE FRENCH ROYAL HOUSE AND ITS FACTIONS

VALOIS

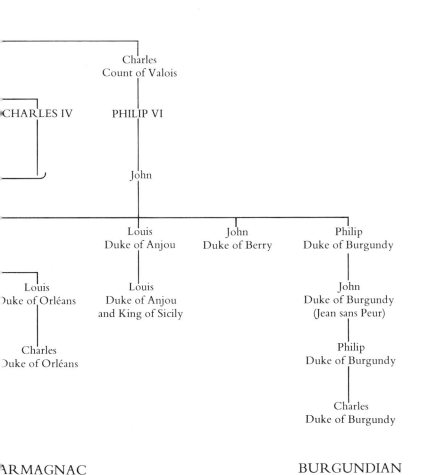

Charles
Count of Valois

CHARLES IV PHILIP VI

John

Louis John Philip
Duke of Anjou Duke of Berry Duke of Burgundy

Louis Louis John
Duke of Orléans Duke of Anjou Duke of Burgundy
  and King of Sicily (Jean sans Peur)

Charles Philip
Duke of Orléans Duke of Burgundy

Charles
Duke of Burgundy

ARMAGNAC   BURGUNDIAN

This story shall the good man teach his son:
And Crispin Crispian shall ne'er go by,
From this day to the ending of the world,
But we in it shall be remembered . . .

Shakespeare: *King Henry V*,
Act IV, Sc. 3

Introduction

When Edward III in 1337 quartered the lilies of France with the leopards of England on his royal standard for the first time, he set in train a series of victories and calamities which historians were later to call the Hundred Years' War. Count Robert of Artois had recently visited the English court with a tale of grievance, having been cheated of his estates by his unscrupulous aunt, Mahaut, and, inspired by such hints of French faction and unrest, Edward decided that the time had come to reclaim his own inheritance. In this he chose to disregard the precedent of Salic Law, a fundamental law initiated by the Salian Franks and other Germanic tribes which excluded females from the inheritance of land, and from which the law excluding females from succession to the French throne derived. It had never applied in England. Edward now proposed to treat the French crown as though it were the English, and enforce his claim which descended to him through his mother, Isabella, 'the She-Wolf of France'.

The moment at which he signified his intent by adding the fleurs-de-lis to his arms and banners and livery was well-judged. Edward's uncle, the last Capetian king, Charles IV, had died at Vincennes without an heir and the throne had been seized by his regent, Philip of Valois. A new French dynasty had begun. As at the birth of all dynasties, the infant was weak and surrounded by close relatives anxious to prove their better claim. France was, as she was to remain for years to come, a cauldron of strife and treachery, of time-serving loyalties and personal greed. She was devoured by faction.

In 1337 Edward III quartered the lilies of France with the leopards of England on his royal standard.

17

Conversely, England's climate was ideal for the procreation of war and conquest.

King Edward was popular, a contrast to his father, the weak and unfortunate Edward II, who, through his passion for power-seeking favourites and general irreverence towards the anointed state, had antagonized his Queen and his subjects alike and had ended as the victim of terrible murder in Berkeley Castle. His heir was strong, able and courageous, and was well supported by his Lords Spiritual and Temporal and by the Commons. The French question had been a thorn in England's side for a long time, ever since the death of Henry II, the Conqueror's grandson, who had married Eleanor, the divorced wife of Louis VII of France. Henry had been Count of Anjou as well as Duke of Normandy, and through his marriage had acquired Eleanor's lands of Aquitaine, Poitou, Guienne and Gascony, vast territories rivalling those of the French king himself. However, by the time Edward III redesigned his royal standard in token of proposed conquest, many of these possessions had been lost. In March 1327 a treaty with France had doomed England to pay a war indemnity. All that now remained to England of Eleanor's possessions was a strip of land running from Saintes in Saintonge and Bordeaux to Bayonne, and a small enclave in Gascony.

The English possessions in France had been a source of constant friction. Indeed, the two royal nations considered themselves natural enemies. By 1337, the tenth year of Edward III's reign, when feudal homage had been asked of English vassals by French lords for lands long since surrendered and even the depleted English holdings were under constant harassment, when a natural antipathy had developed into something more positive under a warlike young ruler, the shame of loss began to smart in English consciousness. All these factors, together with the knowledge that there was no direct royal heir in France, made the time right for war. Lords, Commons, and the Church shared an enthusiasm

Edward III and the Black Prince entering Caen.

En ce io. se leuerent
les anglois bien
matin et sappeil
lerent pour a set
aduers caen. Puis ouyt se
roy messe auat soleil leuat.
Si monta incontment a
cheual et le prince son filz
z messe godefroy de harecot
qui estoit mareschal z gou
uerneur de lost et par quel
conseil se roy ouldroit en
partie. Si se traiuent celle
part seurs bitailles reglees

Si approuchieret la grosse
ville de caen et cheuauchoi
ent les bitailles des ma
reschaulx duant moult
ordonneement. Ceulx de
la ville qui sestoiet mis
aux champs contre les
anglois quant ilz birent
les trois bitailles des an
glois approuchier et seurs
banieres et pennons a gnat
plante et ouyret ces arches
bruyre qlz nauoient pas
acoustumez ilz furent si

The Battle of Crécy, 1346.

which grew over the years, while preparations for a massive invasion went forward, culminating in August 1346. A hand-picked elite of levies estimated at 2400 cavalry, 12,000 archers and other infantry sailed for Normandy, where Edward and his son the Black Prince burned Caen and laid waste all the lands westward of Paris almost to the capital. By this time Philip of France had gathered an army almost three times the size of Edward's own. A challenge was offered; the English force was pushed back to the further bank of the Somme, and the famous encounter of Crécy occurred on 26 August. There for the first time the splendidly arrayed French knights and their Genoese crossbowmen came face to face with that sensational war-machine, the English archer.

The Battle of Poitiers, 1356.

Spectacular though the victory was, the spoils of Crécy were not as great as Edward had hoped. But one prize subsequently fell to him: matchless Calais, his siege of which, by land and sea, lasted almost twelve months. Calais was to remain an English harbour town for the next two hundred years.

By the time of Poitiers, ten years later, the new French king, John, was determined to avenge the defeat of Crécy at a stroke. He recalled the efficacy of the English archer and, knowing that mounted troops could not withstand the hail from the longbows, commanded his armies to march against the enemy on foot. The Black Prince, who was in command of the English force, although trapped and outnumbered, was

*After Poitiers, John II of France was led captive
through the streets of London.*

inspired to order a contingent of mounted knights to a flank
attack while spearguard and axemen went forward into the
heart of the mêlée. The carnage was as great as at Crécy and
the gains far more satisfying. King John himself was captured
and brought as a hostage to London, where his ransom was
fixed at three million gold crowns.

In May 1360 Edward saw his ambitions finally fulfilled. At
the signing of the Treaty of Bretigny England acquired once
more all Henry II's late possessions in Aquitaine; the Ponthieu
inheritance of Edward I; and the whole of the Gascon and
Guienne lands which had been England's at the time of
Edward III's own accession. It was a territory extending far
below Béarn in the far south, eastward to the borders of the
duchies of Bourbon and Berry, and north almost to the River
Loire; a massive acquisition at one point 250 miles across and
300 miles long from north to south.

One might have thought that riches gained so valiantly and
at such cost would have been guarded for ever. It was not to

*Edward the Black Prince, the victor of Poitiers, died
before coming to the throne.*

be: the economic consequences of the Black Death and their culmination in the Peasants' Revolt occupied much of the common consciousness. Edward III fell victim to time and dotage. The victor of Poitiers predeceased him. The House of Valois became established, albeit within a hegemony of cousinly bickering. By 1375 the great French general Bertrand Duguesclin, Constable of France, had pushed the English back into Calais and to meagre strips of land bordering Brittany and Bordeaux. By the time Richard II ascended the throne at the age of eleven in 1377, all the sumptuous possessions – Aquitaine, Poitou, Limousin, Quercy, Rouerge, Marche, Angoumois – had been lost.

Weak, misjudged and martyred, devoid of any conqueror's instinct, and apparently insensible of the hardwon foreign heritage symbolized by his birthplace, Richard of Bordeaux, son of the mighty Black Prince, not only allowed the remaining spoils of war to slip away, even ceding the province of Guienne to France at the Peace of Paris, but took as his second wife Isabella of Valois, daughter of the mad French king, Charles VI. For a brief time a state of precarious amity seemed assured between the two warring nations.

Cousinly bickering, however, was by no means the prerogative of the House of Valois. In 1399 the ambitious Henry Bolingbroke, son of John of Gaunt, rose against his cousin Richard to seize his throne and take his life. By now the English possessions in France were a shadow of what they once had been, and they remained so throughout his reign, for Henry IV had too much to do at home to embark on a French campaign.

For any who cared to look there was one sole ray of comfort. The realm of France was more than ever boiling with faction. A running feud existed there at the time of Henry Bolingbroke's death and the accession of Henry V in 1413. The mad king Charles was a gibbering figurehead who sat unwashed in a threadbare palace convinced that he was made of glass and would shatter at a touch. His effete yet ambitious brother, Louis of Orléans, was seeking to topple the crazed monarch with the help of the Queen, Isabeau of Bavaria, while John, Duke of Burgundy (*Jean sans Peur*), the King's powerful cousin, schemed to outwit them all. Burgundy and Orléans openly or covertly murdered one another's adherents. France was a hotbed of introverted strife, her warring factions preoccupied only with their own supremacy.

It was to this disorderly, elegant, rich, dissolute country that one of the greatest warrior kings in English history was to go forth on a bright August day in 1415. It was to redeem England's honour, and perhaps in secret his own, that Henry V equipped his magnificent force and fleet at Southampton, and he was destined to be remembered with even greater pride and honour than his great-grandfather Edward III, whose martial memory he doubtless revered. His name is synonymous with courage, glamour, and with achieving in military terms the impossible. It is for ever linked to one glittering word: Agincourt.

*Richard II and Isabella at Calais, one of the last
English possessions.*

ye noble and myȝtty Prince excellent
my lord the Prince · o my lord gracious
humble servant and obedient
on to ȝour estate hȝe and glorious
Of whyche I am ful tendre and ful gelous
my recommanñce ynto ȝour Worthynesse
Wyth herte entier and spirit of meeknesse

For me, by Heaven I bid you be assur'd,
I'll be your father and your brother too;
Let me but bear your love, I'll bear your cares.
Yet weep, that Harry's dead; and so will I:
But Harry lives, that shall convert those tears,
By number, into hours of happiness.

SHAKESPEARE: *King Henry IV, Part II*,
Act V, Sc. 2

The King

The singular lack of inclination to make war abroad which England had displayed for a generation was due to be mended in a spectacular manner by the son of Henry Bolingbroke. Bolingbroke's accession had been greeted with mixed enthusiasm and outrage. Archbishop Arundel, a life-long enemy of his murdered and deposed cousin Richard II, had marked the coronation with pompous words:

This honourable realm of England, the most abundant angle of riches in the whole world, has been reduced to destruction by the counsel of children and widows [by which he meant the young Richard II and his mother, Joan of Kent]. Now God has sent a man, knowing and discreet, for governance . . . to act not of his own voluntary purpose or singular opinion, but by common advice, counsel and consent.

These words foreshadowed an unprecedented strengthening of parliamentary power. Just as Bolingbroke, observing feudal privilege, had usurped Richard's throne, the Estates now took it upon themselves to oversee the finances and governance of England in a way that no previous monarch had tolerated. Henry was thus inhibited by his councillors to a time-consuming degree and soon further troubles beset him. The eclipsed faction of Richard II, the wearers of the White Hart badge, spread the rumour that Richard was still alive. The northern marcher lords, led by the old Earl of

Thomas Hoccleve presents De Regimine Principum
to the young Prince Hal.

27

Northumberland and his brilliant son, Hotspur, joined forces with the Welsh, and the exploits of these combined rebel troops occupied Henry for nearly ten years of his reign. Hotspur was killed at Shrewsbury, but Owain Glyn Dŵr, the legendary, almost mythical Welsh princeling who, although hating the English, adhered to King Richard's memory, continued to harass Henry with a series of fierce border raids and independent Parliaments. Northumberland was driven over the border into Scotland but two of his chief confederates, Archbishop Scrope of York and Thomas Mowbray, Earl of Nottingham, were captured and beheaded. Soon afterwards Henry's popularity began to wane, and the Archbishop's execution was likened to that of Becket. At the same time the King's health declined: a vile skin disease, diagnosed by some as leprosy, some as St Anthony's Fire (erysipelas) and some as the wrath of God, achieved what various attempts at assassination by King Richard's Nurslings (as the White Hart wearers styled themselves) had failed to do.

Prominent in Henry's dying thoughts was a planned Crusade to the Holy Land, where the Ottoman Empire still had a firm foothold. Although Richard Cœur de Lion in 1192 had signed a Treaty with the Emperor Saladin which gave the coastal cities of Palestine as far south as Jaffa to the Christian armies and Jerusalem itself was temporarily gained in 1229, the Holy City had been lost fifteen years later, not to be entered again by a Christian army for another seven centuries. Henry Bolingbroke knew of a prophecy that he should 'die in Jerusalem' and had indeed made a pilgrimage there in 1392, but it was actually in the Jerusalem Chamber at the Abbot's Palace in Westminster that his life ended in March 1413. He bequeathed his crusading ambitions to his son, the twenty-five-year-old Henry of Monmouth, Prince of Wales, in whom the dying King's words must have implanted a sense of guilt and obligation. 'What right have you to the crown,

The White Hart, badge of Richard II and of his supporters, known as King Richard's Nurslings.

my son, seeing that I had none?' the King whispered. His son replied: 'Sire, as you have held and kept it by the sword, so will I hold and keep it while my life lasts.' Henry Bolingbroke then said, almost with his final breath: 'Build the walls of Jerusalem, my son.' That instruction was a legacy destined to haunt the victor of Agincourt. It was a knightly quest never to be achieved.

In the mind of the new young king, France came first. Not only as an inheritance seen in terms of lands and perquisites, but France as a total due: her heart, her body, her throne. From the moment he received the sacred oil on brow and breast and hands, it would seem that Henry V considered himself the rightful king of France, and all her subjects his. For had not Edward III styled himself thus?

And again, as in the conquering days of his great-grandfather, the climate of the time was right. England was weary of brawls between Parliament and sovereign, arguments over royal usurpation or rights. The great Welshman Glyn Dŵr was dying, embittered at having failed to achieve supremacy over the English in Wales. There was no longer, in England, the same complex climate of internecine strife. Most of the country's warlike energies were usually channelled into fierce sporadic encounters with the Irish or the border Scots and Welsh. Factions there might be, but these were bred more of feudal loyalty and family squabbles, whereas those of the French were more concerned with the acquisition or tenure, sometimes by interaction with other European dynasties related to the French royal house, of lands and principalities. Moreover, there was a traditional disparity in the way in which French and English monarchs were regarded: Hugh, the first Capetian King of France, had been crowned in 987 by his peers, and the claims of his line were therefore subject to dissent, while William of Normandy had ascended the English throne by right of conquest; few had subsequently thought to question the sovereign right.

After the dreary reign of Henry Bolingbroke, his heir must have presented a romantic figure. Harry of Monmouth had

shown himself in youth to be capable of human error in a
delightfully reassuring way. Although such Shakespearian
stories as that of the young Hal striking Judge Gascoigne in
the face before King's Bench, or Stowe's chronicle depicting
him 'mugging' London citizens by night in company with
his friends can be largely discounted, he evidently led something of a playboy life before his accession. But with the
coming of the chrism, the crown and orb and sceptre, he

*The coronation of Henry V. A detail from his chantry
chapel in Westminster Abbey.*

appears to have become actively and outwardly serious and devout; this made him a more romantic figure still. And physically, in contrast to the scabrous, pustulent monarch recently interred, he must have left little to be desired. Standing on the deck of his flagship at Southampton on 11 August 1415, he looked kingly, comely and competent. More significantly, he was a man with a cause, a dream in which his subjects could share.

Henry, according to his chaplain and chronicler Thomas Elmham, the Cluniac Prior of Lenton, was born in the gatehouse tower of Monmouth Castle on 16 September 1387. The legend goes that his father, who was then Earl of Hereford and Derby, having hurried from Windsor, was being ferried across the River Wye at Walford when he heard of the birth of his eldest son at Monmouth, and was so delighted that he gave the ferryman the monopoly of the ford. Monmouth Castle probably formed one of the fifty manors contained in the large de Bohun holdings around the Welsh Marches, which Henry IV inherited upon his marriage with the heiress Mary de Bohun. (The eleventh-century castle ruins can still be seen.)

Apart from Thomas Elmham's record, Henry's birth went almost unnoticed. No supernatural manifestations such as comets or bloody rain presaged his fame. He was the eldest of four brothers and two sisters, and his mother died at twenty-two, having married Henry Bolingbroke when she was twelve years old. Contemporary portraits show Henry V to be a handsome man, if somewhat lantern-jawed and ascetic. The familiar study reveals a lean, alert profile, direct, dark-brown eyes under delicate brows, a bright complexion (the scar from an arrow-wound taken at the battle of Shrewsbury is not visible), and full, tightly compressed red lips. His hair is severely barbered – a soldier's haircut – and lies like a close brown fur cap above his well-shaped ears. His sharp-nosed

Henry V. From the moment he was anointed, he considered himself the rightful King of France.

face is gaunt from the rigorous physical discipline he imposed upon himself, and the fasting and long rituals of prayer.

This was the King who, at twenty-seven, was setting forth upon the most important campaign of his life: a planned expedition which had become his *raison d'être* and was possibly in itself a private attempt to exorcise unnameable doubts. It is probable that he was more keenly conscious than ever of his father's usurpation after those deathbed words; they lay on him like stigmata. Some time earlier, Henry had had the corpse of Richard II removed from its makeshift tomb at King's Langley, transferring it in splendour to Westminster. As he stood on the deck of his flagship he knew that the twenty-four priests and monks whom he had paid to sing masses for Richard's soul were dutifully chanting around the sepulchre. The attempt at restitution had, however, a dual purpose: by exposing the corpse through the streets of London it was finally established that Richard was indeed dead, thus putting paid to King Richard's Nurslings' attempts to resurrect him in the form of look-alike pretenders.

If the great iron crown of Lancaster sometimes weighed uneasily on Henry's head, he was strong enough to bear it. He was lean and athletic, tallish, straight and active, though it is known that as a child he was gravely ill with some undiagnosed malady. Some of his sporting achievements were prodigious. It was said that he could start, pursue and outrun a deer without the aid of dogs, and wrestle down the beast bare-handed. He had seen active service since the age of thirteen, fighting in Wales and on the borders against Glyn Dŵr's tribesmen at all the principal encounters, living the rough camp existence side by side with veterans. Before King Richard's fall, Henry had been with his expeditionary

OPPOSITE: *On the way to reinterment in Westminster Abbey, Richard II's corpse was exposed to establish that he was indeed dead.*

OVERLEAF: *The future Henry V had accompanied Richard II on his expedition to Ireland and was knighted by him in the field.*

force in Ireland, where Richard had knighted him – an act
that so enraged Henry Bolingbroke that he made a point
later of knighting the boy afresh – and he had been trained
in siegework and all the accomplishments of war: at the
quintain, with axe, mace and bow, mounted with a lance
and on foot with broadsword and knife. He had developed
into a tough, dedicated soldier. Yet he was sensitive, cultured
and artistic. He was meticulous, with a passion for detail and
a retentive memory which stood him in good stead on his
campaigns. He was perhaps more lettered than most noblemen of his time; he could write and speak Latin, and of course
the high French of the court. It is possible that he knew some
Welsh as a result of his birthplace and his campaigns, and his
English, particularly when written, was exemplary for the
times, with all the prepositions spelled right. He was an avid
reader, and invariably seized the library of any captured town.
Among his books was Chaucer's *Troilus and Criseyde*, and he
was patron to Thomas Hoccleve, who dedicated to him his
version of *De Regimine Principum*, and to John Lydgate, whom
he inspired to write his finest poem, *The Life of Our Lady*.

Music was another pleasure: he was adept on the cithera
and the gittern, and from an early age he owned a harp, the
symbol of Wales, with which his own life and later that of
his widow Catherine were linked, in war and love.

RIGHT: *As a young man Henry may have heard
Chaucer reading his works. Music was another pleasure.*
BELOW: *Some fifteenth-century instruments.*

He was deeply religious; according to the *English Chronicle*:

In his youth he had been wild, reckless, and spared nothing of his lusts nor desires, but accomplished them after his liking; but as soon as he was crowned, anointed and sacred, anon suddenly he changed into a new man.

Thus he heard Mass three times daily unless extreme circumstances made this impossible, and had observed long fasts before setting forth on his French expedition. His energy appears to have been phenomenal, for he seldom slept more than five hours a night and was busy with his state affairs by early dawn. He wasted little time during his day, eating whatever meals were put before him without complaint or enjoyment, or fasting for the health of his soul. A man of action and of searing determination, it might be wondered whether some premonition that his great reign would last only nine years spurred him to live it to the full.

That reign had begun in snow, on Passion Sunday, 9 April 1413, when a blizzard unprecedented in men's memory swept over the whole of Europe. While Henry was being crowned King of England and France and Lord of Ireland in Westminster Abbey, farms and villages disappeared in the blank whiteness. Men and beasts perished all over England, gales howled, snow fell unendingly, people became deaf from the icy wind and seers sought portents in the weather. The snow was construed by many as a sign of the new-crowned king's purity. At his coronation feast Henry ate nothing and fasted for three days thereafter. It was evident to all that he was anxious to enter his destiny cleansed and pristine, intent on taking kingship most seriously. Now, on the threshold of his great adventure, he was more sober, more determined, and more wary. Almost on the eve of the departure for France, trusted ministers had shown him their perfidy in a plot which he considered 'most ominous as a presage for the future'.

On Henry V's coronation day a blizzard unprecedented in men's memory swept over the whole of Europe.

King Richard, in the event of his dying childless, had named as his heir apparent the young Edmund Mortimer, fifth Earl of March, who was the great-grandson of Richard's uncle, Lionel, Duke of Clarence, brother of the Black Prince. A secret following had gathered round him, its ambition being to assassinate Henry and replace him with March, who had shown himself to be weak and easily manipulated. The principal conspirators were Richard of York, Earl of Cambridge, the King's cousin and younger brother of Edward, Duke of York, together with Henry Scrope, the King's Treasurer, and Sir Thomas Grey. Also involved was the Lollard Sir John Oldcastle, who planned to raise a rebellion in the West Country, while Hotspur's son, Henry Percy, would act likewise in the north. At the last moment Edmund of March found the thought of this grand design too much for him. Shortly before the embarkation for France, he sought out Henry at Porchester and revealed the conspiracy. Most of the rebels were swiftly captured, tried, hanged, drawn and quartered, but the Earl of March Henry spared, and he had now put on armour to join the expedition as the King returned to his army and the fleet, sailing down the Solent to harbour at Southampton and await the tide for France.

The treachery of Scrope, which appears to have been a family failing – his uncle, the Archbishop of York, having been beheaded for treason against Henry Bolingbroke – was a particularly bitter blow to Henry, for he and Scrope had been close friends in boyhood and adolescence. But another of the conspirators was to be of more lasting significance. Richard of York, Earl of Cambridge, was one of those executed, and he left to his son a legacy of spleen and outrage which was to culminate, long after King Henry's death, in the Wars of the Roses.

LEFT: *The seal of Thomas Beaufort, admiral of Henry V's invasion fleet.* RIGHT: *The seal of the port of Southampton.*

A mighty fighting fleet.

Fair stood the wind for France
When we our sails advance,
Nor now to prove our chance
   Longer will tarry;
But putting to the main,
At Caux, the mouth of Seine,
With all his martial train
   Landed King Harry.

MICHAEL DRAYTON (1563-1631): *Agincourt*

The Company

Henry stood on the flagship named *La Trinité Royale* and nicknamed 'the King's Chamber' and watched the mighty flock of ships come slowly to join her. He had been betrayed; he had acted swiftly and justly as a strong king should. He had prayed for his enterprise to St John of Beverley, to Jesus, Mary and St George. He was purified and prepared, and the long-awaited day was one of golden sunshine. He was naturally moved as he watched his ships, but customarily concealed his emotion. His meticulous eye absorbed all details of the fleet and the faces of those on deck and those coming aboard. The bright August sun gilded ships and faces alike. It was the greatest fighting fleet ever to leave the shores of England.

The decision to go to war had been taken, although for several months negotiations with King Charles had been afoot. These diplomatic skirmishings were, by the very fact of Henry's determination to claim his rights, abortive. In his first letter to Charles he styled himself: 'Henry, by the grace of God King of England and of France.'

To the most serene Prince, Charles, by the Grace of God our very dear cousin. We have endeavoured from our accession to our crown, from the ardent passion that we have had for the love of Him who is the author of peace, to reconcile the differences between us and our people, to chase and banish for ever that sad division, mother of so many misfortunes, cause of the misery of

45

so many men, and of the loss of so many souls which have been
shipwrecked in the slaughter of war . . .

he wrote, protesting 'before God and all men' that he himself
earnestly desired peace. He reminded Charles that 'we shall
have to answer before God for that we retain by force which
rightly belongs to another.'

In a later letter he had declared to Charles:

'We shall propose nothing to you which we have not a
right conscientiously to demand, and we advise you, most
Serene Prince, with all sincerity and from pure love, to entertain those happy thoughts of peace which you have always
observed from your most tender youth, and not to neglect
or abandon them in so mature and advanced an age'. (Charles
was forty-six; Henry, twenty-seven.) 'Reflect,' he begged
the French king, 'upon the years which you have passed.
Think of eternity.'

A French delegation headed by Guillaume Boisratier, Archbishop of Bourges, had come to England in July, with the
message that Charles was willing to submit to the judgment
of Christendom 'whether he had not always wished for peace,
and whether he had not sought it by all just and honourable
means; in proof of which he was willing to dismember his
Kingdom by ceding to England many important territories
and towns and to give Henry his daughter Catherine in marriage with 800,000 gold crowns, a dowry which was unprecedented.'

The terms were not enough. Henry's heritage was clear to
him: not only the territories ceded to Edward III at Bretigny
but the throne of France. All other offerings were null.
Through the Archbishop, he admonished the French King
'in the name of the merciful bowels of Jesus Christ to do us
justice'. It may sound like remarkable hypocrisy when he in-
sisted that Charles would be responsible for 'a deluge of
Christian blood' if the desired terms were not fulfilled, but
to Henry, his cause was unassailable; if he shifted the blame
it was from a rooted conviction of his right. It was bred in
him; he clung to it.

Possibly the final spur had been a remark of the Archbishop prior to his departure back to France:

> Sir, the King of France, our Sovereign Lord, is the true King of France, and with respect to those things to which you say you have a right, you have no lordship, not even to the Kingdom of England, which belongs to the true heirs of the late King Richard. Nor with you can our Sovereign Lord safely treat.

It was the most deadly insult Henry could have been offered. The tabu subject of his father Bolingbroke's usurpation flung Henry into a brief frenzy. He wrote to the Emperor Sigismund and other European rulers begging them to observe that his cause was just. Then his rage cooled, hardening into the determination which had equipped and armed the ships and troops waiting in Southampton Water.

The well-known Shakespearian story (which takes Holinshed's Chronicles as its source) of the Dauphin sending a mocking gift of tennis-balls and eliciting the following words:

> We are glad the dauphin is so pleasant with us.
> His present, and your pains, we thank you for;
> When we have match'd our rackets to these balls,
> We will in France, by God's grace, play a set
> Shall strike his father's crown into the hazard . . .

can largely be discounted as the propaganda of war. Had the Dauphin committed such a bizarre and unchivalrous act, especially at the time when diplomatic negotiations between the two countries were still going forward, it is likely that the talks would have ceased forthwith and the date of invasion been advanced. However, it was a good story with which to inflame the English army.

'The King's Chamber' lay anchored off Spithead, while from every inlet of the coast of Hampshire and east and west along the Solent her sister ships began to move slowly to join the nucleus of the shining fleet. The fifteen hundred ships had taken three days to marshal themselves round their sovereign craft. She was the largest vessel in the English navy and her master, Stephen Thomas, the most skilled and experienced mariner Henry could find, hand-picked like most of his personal staff for the campaign. Lying close to the flagship were other royal craft – the *Katherine de la Tour*, the *Coq de la Toure*, and the *Petite Trinité*, and these had nicknames too such as 'The Wardrobe' and 'The Kitchen', and aboard them were the functionaries for these royal offices. Craft large and small crept under the rhythm of oars to crowd about the flagship. They were beautiful, but *La Trinité Royale* was the loveliest of all. As she moved imperceptibly on the swell of oar-strokes, sunlight gleamed on the gold leaf at her waist and the gilt crown perched over her topcastle. A great gold sceptre bearing three fleurs-de-lis, symbol of the King's main endeavour, was fixed to the capstan. Blindingly bright in the sunshine, a carved gold leopard wearing a silver crown stood at the deckhead. Like many other of the principal craft, *La Trinité* was a four-masted carrack or galleon, her great sails wonderfully and intricately painted. Falcons, antelopes, doves, lions and eagles in blue and scarlet and gold mirrored the devices that decorated her waist, where dragons, serpents, swans and unicorns pranced and coiled and entwined. Her bulwarks were tesselated and criss-crossed with colour, and fastened to them were the shields bearing the arms and emblems of the Household knights, while a row of red pavises – larger shields fixed in close alignment – protected her against bowshot. She was a high-arched ship, graceful as a bird, her poop and prow appearing almost to meet. Countless pennons and ensigns adorned her sails and those of the other craft and were edged with brilliant wind-tossed feathers. Above the masthead of the flagship flew a great banner emblazoned with images of the Holy Trinity. From the rigging streamed a large representation of the Blessed Virgin together with standards showing St George in combat with the Infidel, and St Edward, his hand raised in blessing on the cause. Over all the arms of England and France flowed on the lively air, a painted challenge in blue and scarlet and gold.

As the entire fleet came at last to join the sovereign vessel, men saluting in the fighting-tops above the peacock sails, the masters striking the flag in honour of *La Trinité*, Henry watched in pride, while doubtless remembering the great cost of all this splendour. The equipping of the expedition had brought him near to bankruptcy. While in the Welsh wars he had been forced to pay his soldiers from his own purse, and his household expenses were heavy. Although he drew a revenue of £3000 per year from his Duchy of Cornwall, he was in debt now to the tune of some £7000. To maintain the garrison at Calais he had lately been obliged to pawn some of his jewellery. The old days of feudal military

Jewels such as this fifteenth-century Lancastrian swan badge were pawned to equip the expedition.

service were over. Tenants who held lands by military tenure could be called out for a period of no longer than forty days, and Henry expected his French campaign to last a year. This day of embarkation was the day of muster and from now on the men were the subject of indenture. In other words, the King was responsible for their wages and also the cost of transporting them, their beasts, war-engines and belongings over sea and land. The indentures, which were recorded in the Exchequer at Westminster, were made with various knights, barons and landed gentry who could pledge a certain number of men to fight under their banners, and the wages-scale varied with rank and skill. A duke was paid 13s. 4d. per day (about 67p. in modern currency) – an earl 6s. 8d., a knight

49

Edmundus	Suffolk
Willms	Serlee
Johes	Archebysshop
Willms	Childe
Johes	Emaus
Johes	Vyncent
Thomas	Lunde
Ricardus	Oldsbent
Johes	Dover
Johes	Deince
Johes	Godfrey
Thomas	Grey
Johes	Barry
Johes	Penysads
Johes	Troste
Radulphus	Wadeschike
Willms	Kenyngton
Johes	Lymbury
Willms	Grantham
Johes	Stamdyssh
Johes	Clerk
Ihñs	Thornebury
Johes	Everdon
Johes	Lussh
Georgius	Grafton
Edmundus	Norton
Henricus	Aynt
Johes	Exton
Johes	Halle
Johes	Montgomery
Johes	Plesaunce
Johes	Willy
Henricus	ffowlere
Jacobus	Omdere
Gerardus	Sprongt
Henricus	Sprong
Cedericus	Reignold
Cedericus van	Conghelt
Willms	Ayleston
Ricardus	Hampton
Willms	Mynton
Willms	Harebard
Johes	Bradgate
Michus	Masse
Jacobus	Ince
Hugo	Ince
Petrus	Ince
Karolus	Worsley
Ricardus	Serle
Stevenus	Lokke
Willms	Lokke
Symo	Dothglas
Symo	ffaryngton
Ricardus	Crinler
Ricardus	Wilson
Alexander	Thistle
Johes	Esculle
Michus	Seckes
Thomas	Carson

banneret (a knight of high standing who led others under his own banner, the long pennon of which was squared off to denote its bearer's superiority) 4s., a knight 2s., and men-at-arms and archers had a sliding scale ranging from 4s. to 6d. a day. In civilian life the daily wage of a skilled artisan was 5d. It is difficult to give accurate present-day equivalents of these currencies, but in 14th-century England the ordinary revenue of the Crown (i.e. without parliamentary taxes) averaged £30,000 per annum, knights enjoyed about £60 per annum from their estates, and a ploughman who earned £2–£3 per year ($3·40–$5·40) was doing well for himself.

The muster of the shipping fleet was more arbitrary but no less costly. Commissioners for the Crown were ordered to seize all vessels, masters and sailors in the southern and eastern ports. These included any foreign ships which happened to arrive, among these Dutch, Venetian and Genoese craft, whose crews were accustomed to the role of naval mercenary whether it were in the service of French or English. The vessels thus impressed were held until a service agreement was reached between commissioner and master, who received 3s. 6d. per ton per quarter for use of his ship, the crew being paid in advance.

It was customary to pay the captains a quarter's wages when they made their indentures. Despite generous subsidies from the Commons and the Church, Henry had found himself forced to pawn the greater part of his regalia, some silver, vestments and reliquaries of his own chapel, and a small fortune in crown jewels including the 'Great Harry', a crown pledged to his younger brother, Thomas, Duke of Clarence. The Duke, who had more than a thousand men at muster comprising 240 men-at-arms and 720 horse-archers, found it necessary to break up the crown to pay his officers, who in turn distributed the pledge's value among their waged men. Some of these sapphires, pearls and emeralds were not redeemed for nearly twenty years. The Earl of Salisbury paid

Muster of the retinue of Thomas, Earl of Dorset, captain of Harfleur.

his followers from the proceeds of a silver-gilt ship used as a table-decoration, and Edward, Duke of York took a gold salver embellished with rubies and pearls. Henry even found it expedient to deplete the jewel-coffers of his stepmother, Joanna of Navarre. But there was one piece with which he would not part – his state crown, pure gold with fleurons designed to be worn over his battle-helmet and studded with priceless gems.

One of these jewels, set in the centre of the crown, was the fabulous ruby once belonging to the Black Prince, who acquired it after the fierce battle of Najera in April 1367. The Black Prince had offered his military services to Pedro 'The Cruel' of Castile, who was embattled against his half-brother, Don Enrico of Trastamara. Together with famous captains such as Sir John Chandos and the young John of Gaunt, the Black Prince came from Bordeaux, following Roland's footsteps through the pass at Roncesvalles, and after a severe period of attrition and a bitter struggle triumphed, mainly through the skill of the English archers, over some 16,000 Spanish chivalry. Handsome payment was promised him by Don Pedro but it was never honoured. The only tangible token of Spanish gratitude survived in the magnificent ruby. This can still be seen among the Crown Jewels, set into the Imperial State Crown.

Seagulls screamed and swooped round the mast of *La Trinité Royale*, over the decks and down to forage at the waterline where flotsam bobbed on the swell. The barefoot sailors shouted as they ran across the decks at Stephen Thomas's command. As well as the ships that had been impounded there were many newly built in stout oak from the New Forest and other wooded chases. Below their decks a massive cargo stood cramped in holds. Every vessel carried armaments, armour, victuals, clothing, grain, wine, water and medicines, and, lurching uneasily in tethered lines, were thousands of horses and pack-animals besides stores of baggage-carts. All the ships were crammed to capacity. Despite the fleet's size, it had been impossible to stow all the assembled

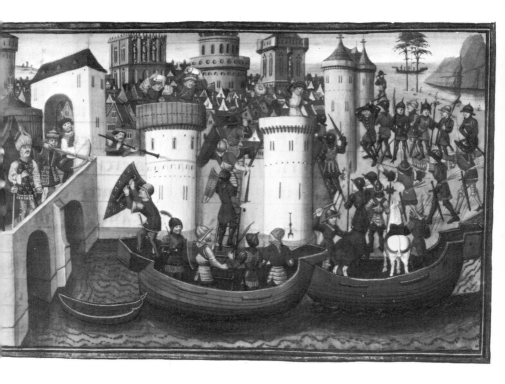

The cargo included thousands of horses and pack-animals.

goods, and arms and horses were left behind on the quay where a great crowd had gathered to watch the fleet set sail.

Lashed to the deckheads and stanchions were the weapons of war. Countless barrels of gunpowder (the export of which had been forbidden since the preparations for war began), casks of brimstone for siegework, and every variety of killing device. Great cannon on which smiths had been working for nearly two years at Bristol and in the Tower of London; cannon balls, enough to sink one ship alone, and three great cast-iron guns: the London, the Messenger, and the King's Daughter. These were twelve feet long and capable of hurling five hundred pounds of stone shot with a roar that alarmed both target and gunners. Crammed above and below decks were less revolutionary but equally cumbersome war-

A bombard, an early form of cannon, which
fired stone shot.

machines. There were ribaudequins – multiple-fire guns with one large barrel for shooting stone balls and several surrounding ones for the discharge of lead pellets; bombardes – cannon weighing only slightly less than the King's Daughter; the eight-foot veuglaires, and the smaller crapaudins and serpentins, all designed to fire a graduated hail of stone.

Adding their weight to all these death-dealers were the countless artefacts and belongings not only of the King but of his principal officers, knights, and the waged men taken aboard the fleet. There were the royal beds, pavilions, chairs and tables, the seals, the state sword, the sets of silver cutlery, the chalices and trappings for the Mass, and even a piece of the True Cross which a Welsh Crusader had brought back from the Holy Land and without which Henry rarely travelled. (There were several hundred such alleged relics going

54

John, Duke of Bedford, the King's brother, was
left in England as regent.

round Europe at the time.) About two thousand knights and
men-at-arms were aboard the fleet – all with their possessions.
Each knight was allowed to bring with him six horses, several
grooms and valets, and personnel such as his scutifer or shield-
bearer whose duty it was to guard the armour and assist his
master in putting it on.

Almost the whole of England's peerage had joined the
campaign, with the exception of lords such as the Earl of
Warwick, who was already in France as Warden of Calais,
the Earl of Westmorland, who was defending the Scottish
borders, the Earl of Devon, who was too old to fight, and
King Henry's brother John, Duke of Bedford, who had been
left behind to act as Regent of England. Two prominent
ecclesiastics were on board: Benedict Nichols, Bishop of Ban-
gor, and Richard Courtenay, the young Bishop of Norwich,

who was one of the King's dearest friends and counsellors and Keeper of the King's Jewels.

Aboard one of the ships was Henry's youngest brother, Humphrey, Duke of Gloucester. Humphrey was a handsome, cultured young man who was later to prove himself courageous in battle and later still, after Henry's death, ruthlessly ambitious. With hindsight one wonders whether, as he stood on deck, he was already envying the royal splendour all about him in the estuary. Unlike Henry, he had suffered no conversion to piety; he was as foppish and licentious as in the old days of the brothers' carefree youth. He loved women, food and wine, and his passion for books, equalling Henry's, was to provide the foundation for the Bodleian Library when Sir Thomas Bodley, whose trimly bearded little statue stands in Merton College Chapel, Oxford, decided after leaving Elizabeth I's diplomatic service in 1598 that: 'In my solitude and surcease from the Commonwealth affayers I could not busie myself to better purpose than by redusing that place (Duke Humfrey's Library) which then in every part lay ruined and wast, to the publique use of students.'

Thomas, Duke of Clarence, the brother nearest in age to the King, was also equipped to sail. France was not new to him. He had led campaigns there three years earlier when he had been created lieutenant in his father's name. On that occasion he had been fighting for one of the French factions, the Orléanists (later styled Armagnacs). They had sought help from Henry Bolingbroke against their mortal enemy, Burgundy, offering tempting bribes (the whole of Aquitaine and a French princess as wife for the then Prince of Wales). The campaign, however, had come to nothing, for by the time Clarence had plundered Normandy and Maine, both factions had, if only temporarily, come to terms. The Duke and his followers were given enough booty to content them, including a magnificent gold cross from a chapel in Bruges

*Humphrey, Duke of Gloucester, the King's
youngest brother.*

Humfroy Dñr de Cloroftia troiziemo mary de Margnelyme de baniere Contesse
de Haymiault

which allegedly contained a nail from the foot of Christ. But now the Burgundy-Armagnac feud was boiling once more. Thomas of Clarence stared out at the wind-freshened sea where the massed ships bobbed and gleamed, and prayed for better fighting than last time. He, though not his brothers, was doomed to be disappointed.

One of the most valuable and experienced knights in the company was the veteran Sir Thomas Erpingham. Tall, wiry and bearded, he had been Chamberlain to Henry Boling-broke and had grown grey in his service and in war. He was a recanted Lollard, and for this reason alone would have been particularly favoured by the devout Henry V, who, as an implacable persecutor of Lollards, must have regarded Erpingham as a brand from the burning; but his particular genius was in the marshalling and training of the 8000 archers at muster this day. He had been fighting almost from the cradle; as a lad in Edward III's later French campaigns and as a man in Wales and Scotland. And he had not forgotten the lessons, read or experienced, the tactics of Crécy and Poitiers. He admired his archers and they respected his stern discipline. He was conscious of their matchless power, knew how to align them to advantage in wedges and diamonds. He could command them to loose or hold their fire, and knew that as one man they would obey.

Edward, Duke of York, lately Earl of Rutland and Duke of Albemarle, waited with others for the tide. A fat, red-faced knight in middle age and partial to the fleshpots, he was still shaken by the recent execution of his brother Richard after the discovery of the Porchester plot. Like the cowardly Edmund of March, the *roi manqué* round whom the conspiracy had revolved, he was glad to demonstrate his relief in combat for the King, whenever and wherever that might be. He had been in trouble himself, at the end of King Richard's reign, being one of Richard's Lords Appellant when Boling-broke had stripped him of his titles. York was a time-server and traitor. Later he had been one of King Richard's Nurslings. During the final rebellion against Henry Bolingbroke which had involved Northumberland, his son Hotspur, Richard Scrope, Archbishop of York, and the Earl of Nottingham, the rebel armies had reached Cirencester, where the populace proved loyal to the king and rose in arms against the Nurslings. There, Edward of York had, without compunction, betrayed his fellow-partisans, even killing a few of them himself. Now the corpulent knight was back in the royal favour, glad not to have involved himself in further conspiracy. He had been married twice, divorcing the daugh-

The arms of Erpingham (left) from the Erpingham Gate, Norwich, and of Edward, Duke of York (right) from a tomb in St Mary and All Angels, Fotheringhay.

ter of the King of Portugal to espouse himself to Philippa, the heiress of John, Lord Mohun.

Thomas, Earl of Arundel had, like the Duke of Clarence, seen service in France three years earlier, but paradoxically had been fighting for Burgundy against Armagnac. The Duke of Burgundy (Jean sans Peur), aghast when Armagnacs ravaged the whole of northern France with a rabble of German and Gascon troops, had appealed for help to England. Led by Arundel and Sir John Oldcastle, the force which arrived was little better than a mercenary troop. A fierce battle was joined at St Cloud, after which Arundel returned home laden with gold ransom from the prisoners he had taken, and less than a year later Englishmen were fighting for Armagnac. At one time, Arundel had held the post of King's Treasurer.

The young Sir John Holland had already been chosen as one of Henry's chief officers. His father, the first Earl of Huntingdon and Duke of Exeter, had – like Edward of York – been stripped of his titles by Henry Bolingbroke for upholding his half-brother King Richard. In his youth, Henry V had

Sir John Holland, later Earl of Huntingdon.

lived in the Earl's forfeited London mansion, Coldharbour. Possibly he was now anxious to make amends, and in any event Sir John was experienced and a good strategist. Sir John was a descendant of that Thomas Holland, first Earl of Kent, who had married Joan, the Fair Maid of Kent, later wife of the Black Prince, and as such was no stranger to tales of war and ransom. His ancestor had fought at Caen in 1346, where he took captive the wealthy Count of Eu, gaining a vast fortune in ransom money.

Sir John Cornwall was another of the hand-picked knight commanders. He had a reputation for courage in the field and diplomacy in council. Along with his contingent of troops he had brought his thirteen-year-old son, who had begged to join the expedition. He was doubtless excited and proud to be acting as scutifer to his father, guarding his baggage, helping him with his armour and, most important, knowing which piece to put on first. Sir John owned the castle of Stepleton, a family manor of the Cornwalls. For his services in France he was later created Lord Fanhope in open Parliament. He was also uncle-in-law to Henry V, having married Elizabeth, Duchess of Exeter (sister of Henry Bolingbroke). Tradition has it that the Duchess fell in love with Sir John after watching his prowess in a tournament. The trophies of Agincourt, including his battle-helm, were kept at Stepleton Castle until the seventeenth century, when they were removed to Burford church. Later they were sold to a blacksmith, who used the helmet for carrying ashes.

Another gentleman, Rowland Lenthall (whose wife was a cousin of Henry IV) provided a contingent of eight lancers and 33 archers for the campaign. He was to be knighted for his services at Agincourt, and with his spoils built Hampton Court in his native county of Herefordshire.

Thomas, Lord Camoys was to play an important part on Crispin's Day. A handsome, able knight, with wide grey eyes and a small moustache, he owned fairly large estates in Sussex and Oxfordshire, where his manor of Stonor lay among sweeping parkland. There, 'the sweetest venison in England' grazed in a meadow which had never been tilled and was rich with thyme and mint and marjoram. At Trotton, Sussex, a memorial to Camoys and his wife can be seen, and Stonor Park was still in the Camoys family in 1977.

Another nobleman who was later to be made Marshal of France was the young Sir Gilbert Umfraville with his Norman name. He was one of the first to set foot in France, and one of the last to die there.

Admiral of the Fleet was the King's uncle, Thomas Beaufort, Earl of Dorset. His ship lay at the mouth of the estuary with two lanterns at her masthead to guide the fleet through

night waters. The Beauforts, bastard sons of John of Gaunt and thus half-brothers of Henry Bolingbroke, had been legitimized by Richard II with the proviso that they never laid claim to England's throne. They had already risen high, and Thomas's brother, Henry Beaufort, was Bishop of Winchester and destined for Canterbury.

Michael de la Pole, Earl of Suffolk, was another who had suffered during the last days of King Richard, whose friend and Chancellor he had been. His lands had been confiscated

LEFT: *Brass of Thomas, Lord Camoys and his wife.*
ABOVE: *Thomas Beaufort, Earl of Dorset* (LEFT), *and Michael de la Pole, Earl of Suffolk* (RIGHT).

by Bolingbroke's council and he had been imprisoned until he had paid a monstrous fine. Now he was ready to set sail under Bolingbroke's son, and had brought his own son Michael with him. Neither would see their homeland again.

Sir Gilbert Talbot, another prominent knight, had been one of the chief officers who had sent out recruiting parties during the past months of preparation. As King's Deputy he had reaped a full harvest of eager men, for the most part young Englishmen ready to serve their king, their minds blazing with thoughts of French plunder and booty, the spoils and ransoms gained at risk to their life.

The father of Sir Thomas Montacute, Earl of Salisbury,
had been one of those murdered by the treachery of the Duke
of York near Cirencester. None the less, Salisbury was prepared to march side by side with York. He was destined to
become one of the greatest campaigners in the ensuing
struggle, capturing over the years vast territories in France.
He was completely dedicated to the service of the King and
of England, as were Lord Fitzhugh, Sir John Greyndon, Sir
Walter Hungerford, Sir Richard Kyghley, Lord de Roos,
and Richard de Vere, Earl of Oxford, who was the son of
King Richard's deposed favourite. They were at one in the
cause, and whether they had supported Richard Plantagenet
or Henry Bolingbroke, the sun was shining on them without
discrimination.

It will be clear from the foregoing that Shakespeare's
famous speech listing the leaders at Agincourt is no model of
accuracy:

> Then shall our names,
> Familiar in his mouth as household words,
> Harry the king, Bedford and Exeter,
> Warwick and Talbot, Salisbury and Gloucester
> Be in their flowing cups freshly remember'd . . .

Although the King, Salisbury, Talbot and Gloucester were
certainly present, Warwick was many miles away at Calais,
Bedford was at home in England, and Exeter (Thomas Beaufort) was not known by that title until some time after the
battle.

In addition to the peers, the men-at-arms and archers, there
was a vast contingent of minor officials whose duty it was to
oil the wheels of this rough life both during battle and in
quieter moments. According to Thomas Rymer's *Foedera*,
written in 1709, there were the artificers such as the hundred
and twenty miners under the command of Sir John Greyndon; their craft was to tunnel beneath the walls of a city under
siege. There were four master gunners, all experienced Dutch-
men, to oversee the operation of the great guns and the
arblasts, bricoles, mangonels, robinets and trebuchets, stone-

hurling devices more archaic but almost as efficient as the King's Daughter; also in their charge were the stores of pitch and oil which could transform the missiles into incendiaries. There was Thomas Fysh with his score of labourers; the fletchers and bowyers such as Robert Mitchell and Nicholas Frost with their underlings; John Flete and his six wheelwrights. Two master carpenters, William Temple and Thomas Matthew, headed a staff of one hundred and twenty. John atte Herst and Robert Berton had brought a contingent of colliers, presumably to mine for sea-coal to fuel the army.

In total there were about 500 labourers and artisans, each man a member of his particular Guild, most craftsmen bringing their apprentices. Although the single-hearted climate of the day allowed little room for class discrimination and every man was valued for his skill, there was an elite hierarchy distinguishing itself by being in the King's service. There was John Covyn, Sergeant of the King's Tents and Pavilions, with his twenty-eight yeomen. Nicholas Colnet, physician, came with a retinue of three archers. John Waterton, esquire, was Master of the King's Horse and brought with him sixty grooms. Nicholas Harewode was Clerk of the Stable and Gerard de la Strade was personal groom of the King's chargers and ponies. Guy Midelton and John Melton held the offices of King's Guide by night. Cofferer of the royal Household was William Kynwolmersh. Thomas Harvey was one of eight Servitors to the King. William Heryot with others was Messenger of the King's Chamber, and John Bromley was Groom of the same. Estephin Payn was the Almoner, and Thomas Bridde his sub-almoner. The ecclesiastical contingent included Master Edmund Lacy, Dean of the King's Chapel, and thirteen chaplains, among them Thomas Elmham, chronicler of the battle to come. There were several friars, headed by Alain Hert and John Brotherton.

Yeomen from every department of the King's Household were on board: Norman Synford of the King's Poultry, Nicholas Burcester with eight yeomen of the Bakehouse; William Balne, Clerk of the Kitchen; and his under-clerks of

Kitchen, Pantry and Buttery. In charge of the table-linen, the cloth of Damascus napkins, was Jacob Meyndy, Yeoman of the Napery. With the keys of the spice chests at his belt was Walter Burton. There were fifteen clerks of Scullery and officials of Bakehouse and Hall. John Feriby and Thomas Morton ruled over the Wardrobe and under them were yeomen designated Archers of the Wardrobe. Other craftsmen were George Benet, Master Cordwainer, with twenty-six other cordwainers or shoemakers.

It would be impossible to enumerate or name all the vast community crowding aboard the fifteen hundred ships. All were masters of their trade and most were capable of attack and defence if necessary. The national pastime of archery had become a statutory skill since the Statute of Winchester issued during the reign of Edward III. Practice at the butts had become compulsory. Even the ecclesiastics had their attendant bowmen and a fighting archbishop, for example the Archbishop of York, William de la Zouche, was far from unknown. De la Zouche had fought as one of the leaders at Neville's Cross in October 1346, against an invading army of Scots led by David II, son of Robert the Bruce. David's army was defeated and he himself taken prisoner, while Scotland's principal holy relic, the Black Rood (a reliquary containing

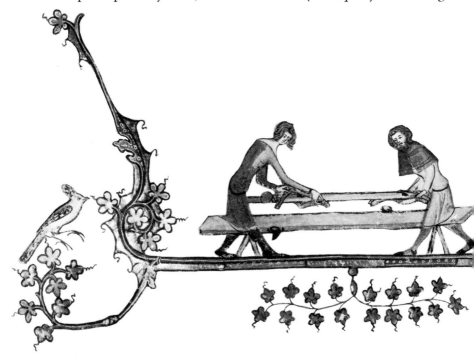

a piece of the True Cross) was seized and brought to England.

The surgeons, Thomas Morestede and William Bradwardyn, brought a large staff and medicines by the sackful; coffers of herbs, knives and saws for amputations, leeches and irons to let blood from men probably already weakened by its loss. Rolls of linen bandages, salves made from the juice of flowers, and the only anaesthetic, tincture of poppy, which it was hoped would induce drowsiness during surgery. There were smiths and saddlers, tentmakers and men such as Nicholas Brampton, whose function was described as 'Stuffer of Bacynets' (wadding the helmets with cotton or flax to prevent chafing). There were baggage-boys, little more than children, to guard the horses and gear while their masters went on foot into combat. There were light horsemen called hobelars who could be used as messengers and spies. At the other end of the scale were the royal heralds: Leicester, Guienne, Ireland King of Arms, Chester Herald, Antelope Pursuivant, and Hereford Marshal of Arms, all of whom owned diplomatic immunity and would be sent to offer challenges and parley for terms before or during a battle.

There were the armourers. Under the ægis of one Allbright Mailmaker, skilled men had care of the thousands of pieces of plate and chain mail and the countless weapons, the swords,

Artificers at work: polishing and grinding a sword.

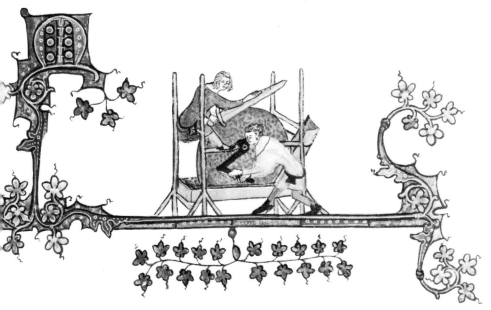

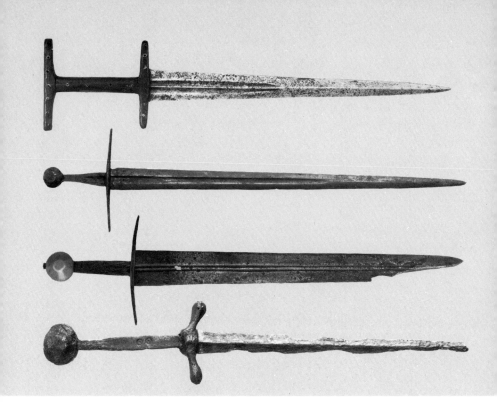

Swords, useful for head lopping and often used in a
two-handed grip, and daggers for stabbing and striking
in close combat.

lances, knives, poleaxes and mauls and maces, and the little
killing-daggers known ironically as 'misericords' which could
be slipped between the joint of an adversary's mail and into
his vitals. With oils and sand and hidecloth Mailmaker's men
repaired and cherished, forged and hammered and honed the
blades and bardings of iron and copper and fine Nuremberg
steel. The hundred-year-old Assize of Arms stipulated that
each commissioned officer should present himself *'bien mon-
tez, armez et araiez comme a leur estatz ils appartient'* – mounted,
armed and arrayed as befits his estate.

During the latter part of the fourteenth century and the
early fifteenth, the style of armour had changed as experi-
mentation took place. The chain mail hauberk worn at Crécy

'A Milanese bascinet with mobile visor and chainmail aventail, and various offensive weapons.

and Poitiers gradually gave way to jointed plate armour. Fighting men still wore the *jacque* (also called a *gambeson* or *cotte gamboisée*) which was a quilted tunic of *cuir bouilli* (boiled leather moulded to the wearer's shape and stuffed for added protection with silk flock or cotton), but over all metal plates of varying thicknesses and measurements were strapped or riveted together. An alternative form of armour was the brigandine, pieces of smaller plate-mail overlapping one another like fish-scales and forming a garment which covered the wearer from neck to hips. These brigandines were fairly pliable and resistant to arrow or sword. In a typical example at the Tower of London, the plates are made of thin iron, one inch square, pierced by grummet-like holes, or eyelets,

Bombards and crossbows in action during a siege.

through which the fastening cords passed. Other types of brigandine had their plates covered with small studs, presumably to deflect missiles. A long surcoat known as the cyclas became obsolete with the coming of plate armour, but the men, especially knights banneret and bachelor, wore over their harness a light jupon or tabard upon which were displayed their armorial bearings.

Steel from Nuremberg was highly prized, but the finest and swiftest workmanship came from Milan. The two greatest families of armourers were the Negroli and the Missaglia. Such was their prestige that in 1435 Tomasso Missaglia, having made armour for countless knights, was himself knighted for this service. By the early fifteenth century Milanese craftsmen boasted that they could supply armour for four thousand cavalry and two thousand infantry within a few days, and most of Henry's fighting elite was equipped from this source. A burnished helmet (the bascinet) was worn with a protective nose-piece and mobile visor, sometimes grotesque, but without the plumed crest or panache, this being reserved for tournaments. Much of the face was left exposed so that reasonable vision could be obtained in combat.

A man's body was more or less completely encased. Below the steel hauberk legs were covered by greaves, leg-guards jointed at knee and ankle which met shoes of reticulated steel. The arms were similarly clad in steel plates with protruding elbow-guards and pauldrons on the shoulders. Gussets of chain mail were used to protect the plate-joins at armpit and knee, and chain mail aventails, falling from the base of the helmet, shielded the nape of the neck and the chin. About the waist was worn the baldric, an ornamented sword-belt through which an axe, dagger and pole-axe could also be thrust. Hands were clothed in heavy gloves of boiled leather or velvet and outer steel gauntlets were studded with iron gadlings, which gave a knuckle-duster effect. To harness a man-at-arms thus was a lengthy and complicated process learned painstakingly by the grooms and apprentices. Each piece must go on in the right order – for instance if the greaves were strapped on the legs before the steel shoes, the latter could not be fitted. Despite the intricacies of this harness, every suit was fashioned to give the maximum flexibility, and some knights could achieve the same mobility as soldiers in full pack who marched in the 1914-18 War. The patron saint of armourers was naturally enough St George, who was invariably depicted spearing the Dragon.

A variety of weapons abounded. The chased and embossed swords worn by the elite corps were useful for head-lopping and were often used in a two-handed grip, but in close combat there would be little opportunity for showy swordsmanship or the balletic cut-and-thrust that was a feature of the tournaments. Experience had shown that the most orderly battle-line would deteriorate to some degree into a scrimmage, when a man-at-arms might depend on quick stabbing, bludgeoning or lancing. So he carried his short strong knife, his mallet or pole-axe and a wooden lance ten or twelve feet long, headed by a metal glaive. Also used was the halberd –

a double-edged spear and battle-axe combined, the maul or lead truncheon for the beating out of brains, and a billhook, effective in disembowelling an unarmoured enemy. Flemish mercenaries had been recruited into the ranks, their favourite weapon being a six-foot pike, its heavy steel head capable of impaling a fallen foe into the ground. Like all the ordinary foot-soldiers, these mercenaries were more lightly armoured than the noblemen-at-arms. Their brigandines and the sallet on their heads weighed less than the knights' elaborate armour. None the less they carried some forty-five pounds of steel and their mobility was rationed, most of their attacking force being delivered from behind a shield of pavises set into the ground.

The destriers or war-horses, finest bloodstock bred for the purpose, could cost a knight up to £100 each. In the past it had been customary to arm them with 'bards' of plate mail which protected face and hindquarters, but by the time of this campaign the practice had been largely abandoned. The strength of a cavalry charge lay in its speed, a fact recognized nearly fifty years earlier by the Black Prince at Poitiers. Also it was becoming more and more customary for an army to fight dismounted. Even so, there was an abundance of mounts aboard. Every duke had an entitlement of fifty horses, an earl had twenty-four, a knight six, an esquire four and a horse-archer one. Together with the pack-animals and the beasts owned by the clerks and artisans, the number that sailed from Southampton could not have been less than 25,000.

Not all the men at muster were English; apart from Flemings there were Gascon mercenaries and some Genoese foot-soldiers had come to join the affray with their specialized weapon, the crossbow. This Italian-made device was not popular in England and was becoming obsolete with good reason. It fired 'quarrels' of iron and steel (the name derives from the French carré, the heads of these bolts being four-sided), but although these could pierce a target at over four hundred yards, the process of loading was extremely cumbersome. The crossbow weighed between fifteen and twenty pounds; a hook linked to the bowman's belt had to be passed round the bowstring, the bow itself being held by a foot in a stirrup on the ground while the string was latched behind another hook which held it until the discharge of fire. Other intricacies of its handling included gaffles and winders, screws and pulleys, according to the type of bow used. Although heavy missiles known as garrots and viretons (wrapped in blazing tow) could be fired, long seconds were needed to re-load. For all that, it was still a favourite weapon of the French, who perhaps admired its complexities.

At the other extreme, there was as in every Continental army a large contingent of Irishmen, whose only weapons were an enormous knife and a bundle of short throwing-spears. Small, wild and bearded, permanently in love with war and death, they disdained even the most elementary trap-pings of protection. Wearing little more than a loincloth, tat-tooed with ancient tribal markings, they swarmed above and below decks. Their ancestors had worshipped the Morrigan, the old goddess of battle, and they were still so sure of her shield that they were content to run naked into combat.

Lastly there were the archers, the heart of the army, her honour and her core. The six-foot Welsh longbow, the dead-liest, swiftest and most efficient of weapons, was tried and victorious, first in the Scottish campaigns of 1334, then at Crécy and Poitiers. Yew trees were traditionally the best source of production and to prevent the decimation of sup-ply, bowyers were instructed to make four weapons of ash, wych hazel or elm to every one they made of yew. At times the yew – *Taxus baccata* – was imported from Spain. The secret was in the grain of the wood, the blend of sapwood and heartwood which gave the bow an extra vibrancy and re-sponse. Razor-tipped steel headed the arrows, and their shafts were fletched with goose or duck or peacock feathers and sometimes flights of parchment. In the hands of a skilled archer the longbow could discharge ten or twelve arrows per minute as against the crossbow's two. With reasonable vision and a practised hand, the bowman could score a hit through chain mail over 275 yards, and the shafts were capable of piercing a four-inch oak door.

The bowmen were the most lightly armed of all. As their weapon was essentially a defence against advancing cavalry, they were always dependent upon a suitable terrain and mobility was vital. Therefore they wore a short-sleeved *jacque* (the shirt of boiled leather, sometimes scantily reinforced with mail), breeches and light leather shoes, and leather gloves to protect their hands and wrists from the bowstring. Their heads were covered with a wickerwork bascinet crossed with iron. Generations of practice at the butts in villages and towns had taught them the correct use of weight and strength, the notch, the stretch, the loose, the leaning of the whole weight into the horns of the bow; they were experts. Ancient statutes compelled them to have their gear always ready – clothing as described, together with a sword, dagger and poleaxe which were thrust through the belt, and some forty or fifty arrows; not all were issued with a quiver.

These were the yeomen archers from Kent and Sussex and

Archers with the longbow, and crossbowmen.

the Midlands, from every shire in England as far as the Scottish border. Towards the end of the previous century the chronicler Froissart had written:

> Prowess is so noble a virtue that one must never pass over it too briefly, for it is the mother stuff and the light of noble men and, as the log cannot spring to life without fire, so the noble man cannot come to perfect honour or to the glory of the world without prowess.

Philosophies such as this, coupled with a regard for England's honour, had brought the men willingly indentured. Not only Englishmen had come flocking to the royal standards and to the bannerets of their knights commander. The originators of prowess such as this, the chief exponents of the longbow, were there in force. The Welsh had left their valleys and cantrefs to follow Henry of Monmouth, Prince of Wales.

There was Dafydd ap Llywelyn ap Hywel (Davy Gam), brother-in-law to the great Glyn Dŵr who even now lay dying, and veteran like him of fierce border raids, sieges and battles, at Grosmont, Craig-y-Dorth and Harlech. A black

*Indentures for jewellery loaned to the King. The top
one is Davy Gam's.*

patch covered an eye lost in one of these battles against the
hated English; the other eye winked out, cynical yet in
grudging, delighted anticipation. He admired the English
king. Prince of Wales he might be, the title claimed by Glyn
Dŵr as his own, but Dafydd remembered the good fighting
in Wales against the boy prince, just as he recalled Glyn
Dŵr's cause with affection and regret. And now a general
amnesty had been declared to all rebel Welshmen who would
join this campaign.

With Dafydd ap Llywelyn ap Hywel came a great wave
of clansmen and kinsmen, many related by blood, few speaking anything other than Welsh, their minds attuned to fighting, if not for the English king, in secret for their own honour
and that of Wales. Their commanders assessed their strange-

76

ness, their tilted eyes of a bloodline used to lifting them to the mountains for generations past; their wild, set, singing faces; their imaginations whipped to a war-frenzy for years by the bloodthirsty chanting of the bards. Some had come at the bidding of English barons, the marcher lords who held Crown tenure in Wales, but those from independent territory had come secretly, disobeying guardians who clung to old resentments. All Wales had yielded them up: from Ruvoniog, Kimmerch, from Dyffryn Clwyd, from Mold in the Alun valley, from Chirk, from Pembroke, from Pool, Powys and Kerry, from Clun, Wigmore, Radnor, from Talgarth and Blaenfllyfni, from Gwenllwg, from the twenty-four minor lordships of Over Went and Nether Went, and from the Honour of Monmouth. For them, life would never again be so new. Among the young volunteers was one Owen ap Meredyth ap Tydier, who later through his liaison with King Henry's widow, would be revered as the founder of the Tudor dynasty and the great-great-grandfather of Elizabeth I.

From the King down to the smallest Irish desperado, the cosmopolitan company's mind was fixed on ransoms. In the foreign country they now anticipated invading everything or almost everything was forfeit. The perquisites were boundless. Valuables were fair game to lords and commoners alike, with the proviso that permanent structures arbitrarily belonged to the King, who was entitled to one-third of all booty and the persons of any French royal hostages he might capture. Otherwise all movables in the army's path were legal spoil. The old tales went round of selling back wealthy prisoners to their families and returning enriched for life from the wars. Even civilians were unprotected; an army on the move often had the chance of capturing a rich merchant and bigger fish were to be had. The traditional antipathy which existed towards France was fanned by recollections of French raids during the last ten years, when Plymouth and the Isle of Wight had briefly been invaded.

The rules regarding booty and ransoms were complicated. Officers were entitled to one-third of the plunder taken by

their men, and syndicates, approved by the commanders, were formed in the ranks in order to rob the enemy more efficiently. A thorny issue customarily arose over the legal capture of hostages. In a mêlée it was difficult to swear exactly whose right hand first seized the captive's right gauntlet (the accepted terms of capture) and cumbersome lawsuits, sometimes lasting for years, often ensued. Also, the prisoner had merely to say 'I yield' and the subsequent rush to guard the prize in a safe place sometimes put the battle's outcome in jeopardy. None the less, ransom raged in the thoughts of the army, and ransom they would have.

Henry had issued stern edicts regarding the conduct of his troops in France. He visualized himself as the instrument of God, for, once the campaign was over and he with divine help victoriously restored to his rightful heritage, his struggle against the Infidel could begin. The thought of Jerusalem was an omnipresent spur. Therefore nothing must be done to debase God's cause. At the time of indenture, all men connected with the enterprise had been warned that churches and the persons of priests, nuns and monks must be left unmolested. Any man caught despoiling a holy place or laying hand upon a sacred vessel would be summarily hanged. The Holy Sacrament was to be revered as at home. Women were to be respected (an ambitious declaration on Henry's part for an enemy's women were by tradition destined for rape) and any man harming a pregnant woman or endangering the life of her child was to be put to death, or at best:

> to lose all his goodes half unto him that accuseth him, and half unto the Constable and Marshall, and himself to be dede but if the King gave him his grace.

The army's morals too were to be guarded; no women came aboard the fleet. The usual camp followers were banned,

Part of a muster roll showing the names of archers supplied by the Duke of Gloucester.

and it was decreed that any harlot coming within three miles of camp should have her left arm broken. Even swearing was forbidden – an impossible veto among the thousands of men, but one observed if only in the royal presence. Repeatedly Henry assured the army that the cause was sacred, and a suitably puritan band was leaving England's shore.

The tide was almost right for sailing. The master mariner Stephen Thomas cast an anxious look along the deck of the *Trinité* at his sovereign, who stood gazing at the quay where among the crowd his stepmother, Queen Joanna, watched amid a score of priests chanting for the success of the voyage.

It was mid-afternoon on 14 August 1415 when the first vessel nosed into the estuary and dropped anchor.

The time had come. He raised his hand to the master and a trumpet sounded, its call taken up from ship to ship along the stretch of water to where the Admiral's craft lay. The chanting of Queen Joanna's priests grew louder and was echoed by the chaplains aboard the fleet. Henry had said his own prayers long ago, making large offerings at St Paul's, and had made his will, in which he remembered not only great councillors but those such as Joan Waring, his ancient nurse, and which ended:

> This is my last will, subscribed with my own hand, H.R. *Jesu Mercy and Gramercy. Lady Marie help!*

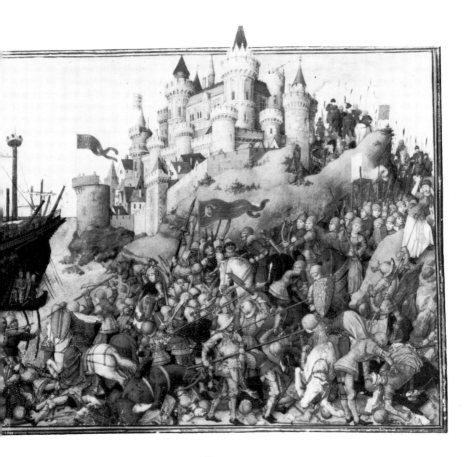

The great convoy of ships began to close up as they saw the flagship's mainsail hoisted to half-mast. Bright sunlight picked out the gilded ornaments on the body of the fleet and a north breeze blew the fringed pennons and banners and filled the radiant sails. A flock of swans flew overhead. Drums beat; the clarions screamed. Look-outs clung like spiders to the rigging, and sailors hauled lustily on the staysails. Richard Courtenay, the King's beloved Bishop, intoned a psalm for deliverance. And then a minor catastrophe occurred. Upon one of the Dutch vessels, a ship impressed and paid for at some cost, a brazier tipped with the lurch of the deck. In moments fire raged. There was gunpowder aboard – an explosion set alight two other ships nudging close by. Men shouted and fought the flames and dived overboard. The horses screamed in the pitchy darkness. Aghast, the royal commanders watched while the three ships burned down to the waterline and scorched men and beasts swam frantically in the harbour. Whispers arose; a bad omen.

Henry was undeterred. Omens or no omens, he would never turn back; it was not his way. The afternoon tide was full, the wind was right. The sun was bright on the still glorious fleet, on the faces of dukes and earls, priests and artisans, the foreign mercenaries, the loyal English yeomen and the mystic Welsh with their priceless longbows, the little wild Irish. Upon the lords the light shone, blinding them to old grudges and gilding their single-heartedness. Upon the great guns and siege-engines it swept and flickered with the growing breeze, and it warmed the close-cropped soldier's head of Henry of Monmouth, Prince of Wales, Knight of the Bath, Duke of Cornwall, Earl of Chester, Duke of Lancaster and Aquitaine, and King of England – and France. Slowly Admiral Beaufort led the great armada out to sea. It was about three in the afternoon on Sunday, 11 August 1415. Young knights lined the decks to wave farewell across the widening strip of water to the quay. One hundred and fifty years later, Michael Drayton immortalized the scene in *The Barrons' War*:

One wore his mistress' garter, one her glove;
And he a lock of his dear Lady's hair;
And he her colours, whom he did most love;
There was not one but did some favour wear;
And each one took it, on his happy speed,
To make it famous by some knightly deed.

*The swan was one of the badges of the house
of Lancaster.*

And to the town of Harflew there he tok the way
And mustred his meyne faire before the town,
And many other Lordys I dare well say,
With baners brighte and many penoun;
And there they pyght there tentys a down,
That there embroudyd with armys gay;
First, the Kynges tent with the Crown,
And all other Lordes in good aray.
    Wot ye right well that thus it was.
    Gloria tibi trinitas!

JOHN LYDGATE (1370–1450) attr.: *The Bataille of Agincourt*

The Siege

The madness of King Charles VI of France was intermittent and yielded sometimes to long periods of lucidity. Perhaps the prospect of Henry's invasion, coming now in tangible form across the Channel, restored the royal sanity for a while. In Paris he had begun to take heed of the thread to his sprawling, disorderly realm. With him was his son, the nineteen-year-old Dauphin Louis, a youth much given to women and wine, and he too was moved to marshal a force against the invader. The Archbishop of Bourges had returned with news that the final terms had been rejected, and the royal house and the warring factions of Burgundy and the Orléanist Armagnacs began in their separate ways to respond to the now inevitable challenge.

The feud still raged; in fact Burgundy was more cordial to the invading English king than to its own warring cousins. While the peace negotiations were still in progress Burgundy as well as Armagnac had offered its own terms to Henry, going over the head of the French royal house to suggest that he be content with the lands due from the Treaty of Bretigny. But by that time Henry had widened the scope of his ambition. His sights were set first on Normandy, which he con-

*Christine de Pisan presents her work to Charles VI
of France.*

85

sidered his Duchy through his ancestor, William the Conqueror. His plans, however, he communicated only to his principal war councillors, telling them exactly where he planned to anchor the fleet.

Although the Dauphin Louis had been appointed Captain-General of all military personnel, he was powerless to control the strife between the two great dukes and their vassals. Unlike the fighting force that had left England, there was no singleness of purpose in France; the blood-debts and grudges were too strong. Less than a decade earlier Louis of Orléans, the Dauphin's uncle, had been murdered in the night streets of Paris by the agents of Jean sans Peur, Duke of Burgundy. Charles, the young son of Orléans, had married Bonne of the Armagnacs, daughter of the powerful Count Bernard, and with this alliance an even stronger faction had been formed, its members howling for Burgundy's blood. Jean sans Peur, customarily cool and far-sighted, kept himself somewhat aloof from the English threat. He waited, holding his armies in abeyance, hoping to see Armagnac destroyed by the foreign power.

Fortunately for France, there were several great generals and commanders more sensible of the dangers and anxious to present an armed defence – men who were skilled in combat and great landowners of noble blood who had no desire to see their territories laid waste. Soldiers like Jean Boucicaut, the Marshal of France, a famous jouster and military campaigner who favoured delaying Fabian tactics rather than a pitched battle. He had fought with the Teutonic Knights in Prussia, and later against the Turks at the battle of Nicopolis, from which he alone of his small force returned home. There was Charles d'Albret, Constable of France, a brave fighter and also an experienced strategist, and the Sire de Rambures, one of France's best artillery commanders. There were men yet uncommitted, like the Dukes of Brittany, Berry, Alençon

Jean sans Peur, Duke of Burgundy, kept somewhat aloof from the English threat.

87

and Bar, and the Counts of Fauquemberghes, Eu, and Robert
de Bar, Duke of Marle; likewise the Counts of Richemont
and Vendôme, Duke Edouard de Bar, the Counts of Granpré
and de Roucy, Ferry de Lorraine, Count of Vaudémont,
Jean de Bar, Sire de Puisaye, and Jacques de Châtillon, Seigneur de Dampierre. There were also men like Philip of
Burgundy, Jean sans Peur's eldest son, who was doomed to
be forbidden the affray by his father, and Antoine, Duke of
Brabant, who would join it too late. Rich, knightly and
chivalrous, these were the men who, as Henry's fleet approached his chosen harbour, went swiftly or slowly to gather
a force, to argue against fighting in collusion with a hated
kinsman, or simply, like the Duke of Burgundy, to watch
and wait.

Meanwhile the royal tax-gatherers began to sweep down
on the French populace, much to its chagrin; some of the
country at least was arming, and those who put on harness
did so magnificently, with the panache indigenous to French
pride. They owned the best horses, the most elaborate
armour, the brightest blazons. Such pride was an inherent
part of them. Although the English might have let all their
great gains in France slip away, there was still the smarting
memory of Crécy and Poitiers to be expunged once and for
all, and the knights now sending for their brilliant armour
and gay tabards remembered old tales of war and tactics, and
the matchless Fabian strategies of the late great Bertrand
Duguesclin.

He had been one of the most magnificent commanders in
French military history, and perhaps the best loved. The son
of a Breton nobleman, he had soldiered unremittingly in
France and Spain for thirty years, always loyal to the Crown
of France, and had received the highest accolade, that of
Constable. He had died in 1380 while on campaign at
Châteauneuf-de-Randon, and his last words to his officers

*Jean Boucicaut, Marshal of France, shown here
with his wife.*

were to make war only on those carrying arms, and that women, children and churchmen were not their enemies.

Those of the French chivalry who prepared for war pressed into their ranks foot-soldiers and bowmen who, unlike the English troops, showed a certain unwillingness to fight for their country – not so much through lack of patriotism as because there was not the same stable system of indenture and payment of wages as in Henry's army (some were lucky to be paid at all). As with their overlords, little grudges and loyalties ruled, and the ducal feud was mirrored in the ranks. Their differing colours warred and discipline was extremely difficult to maintain, while aboard the fleet now sailing steadily towards the Normandy coast, every man at muster wore the emblem commanded by Henry and the bloody cross of St George shone from rich mantle and coarse wool jerkin alike. Led by the Earl of Dorset, the convoy, its painted sails bulging tightly under the fair wind, moved towards the port of Harfleur.

As in 1944 when the Allied Armies landed in France, it was fully expected that Henry would strike at Boulogne, so that this and other coastal towns were hastily being fortified, while a Flemish patrol was vigilant from Nieuport to Sluys. But Henry had chosen Harfleur as the principal gateway to Normandy and thence to his ultimate goal of Paris, for although Bordeaux was still an English possession, he estimated it would have been madness to invade either in the south-west or in the Seine valley. It was essential that the initial landing should take place south of Calais and preferably at an important port not too far from the capital; Harfleur fulfilled these conditions. It was a beautiful little town, famous for ship-building, weaving and dyeing, and notorious for smuggling and piracy. And it was heavily fortified.

Sitting astride the river Lézarde and built on a marsh, Harfleur was circled by a wall two and a half miles in circum-

*Jean, Duke of Berry, veteran of Poitiers, fought
at Agincourt.*

ference, with a wide moat outside the wall which was pierced by three gates – the Leure gate in the south-west, the Rouen gate in the south-east and the Montivilliers gate in the north-east. Drawbridges protected the gates, and along the wall were twenty-six towers, decorated with gaudy statues, dragons, snails and birds, and pierced by slits and embrasures for the discharge of missiles against a besieger. It was mid-afternoon on 14 August 1415 when the first vessel, a ship commanded by Sir John Holland, nosed into the estuary three miles west of the town and dropped anchor at the Chef de Caux, where Le Havre now stands. The sun still shone brightly, lighting the rich blue and gold of the carved devices on the towers of Harfleur. Eyes watched from behind the fortifications and an immense barbican of iron-bound timbers which protected the Leure gate. The other gates faced across the river or the marsh, which the garrison commander had earlier ordered to be flooded. Adding to the hazards were stakes and tree-trunks which had been driven deep into the swollen water of the moat. Harfleur sat quietly, seeming im-pregnable, while the English fleet lay just as quietly at the Chef de Caux and the summer evening gathered. Henry un-furled the royal banner at the masthead of the *Trinité* for a council of war. His cousin the Duke of York was summoned, and his brothers Humphrey of Gloucester and Thomas of Clarence, with eight earls and two bishops. The meeting was brief. The King issued his orders: the fleet was to lie at anchor all night, and at dawn a reconnaissance was to be made by Sir John Holland, Sir Gilbert Umfraville and Sir John Corn-wall. All troops were to stay on board. He reiterated his edicts: no plunder, no molestation of the peasants in their hovels outside the town, no women, no excesses. That the cause was God's was still his paramount thought; also, such a stern discipline served to maintain stability within the army. Moreover, he judged that Harfleur was by right his town, the

Henry issued his orders: the fleet was to lie at anchor all night.

Here sheweth. howe after the cummyng home of Erle Richard, from the holy lande
wy the 2th then beyng kyng of Englond was secretely enformed of a preuey and
pryn insurrecion of trackerous heretikes which sodenly by myght purposed to haue
one kept the kyng endes then rule a subiecion / and after by his auenens to haue
troubled the chirch of Englond / and to slee the prelate and distribute theyr possessi
ens the hous of god / after theyr indiscrete advises and pleasure

citizens his people who should be respected accordingly. The word was passed, the men lay down to sleep. The garrison tower of Harfleur maintained silence. And from the marsh arose a stench in the warm evening, a putrid stink of salt, rotting vegetation and rancid shellfish that the army would grow to hate during the long days ahead.

The reconnaissance made by the three knights next morning revealed a deserted beach littered with rocks, and no sign of life from the guarded town. Swiftly the business of unloading men and horses, armaments and supplies from the 1500 ships went ahead. The operation took three days, during which Henry celebrated the Feast of the Assumption of the Blessed Virgin. His pavilion, tasselled and crowned with bright banners, had been set up, together with those of the other lords. His chaplains said the daily offices, Snaith Fidler and his minstrels played psalms and motets; life in the royal tents proceeded as calmly as at Westminster. Meanwhile Henry meticulously oversaw the details of the disembarkation, establishing a line of outpost guards between the army and the town in case the garrison should break their stillness and attack the troops unloading provisions and siege-engines from the beached rafts and boats.

Within the garrison there were in fact only 400 troops, under the command of the Sire d'Estouteville, who by this time was fully cognizant of the English manœuvres and the approximate number of the army near the Chef de Caux. That number might have perturbed him more had he not been confident of Harfleur's reinforced defences – the barbican, the marsh made scarcely fordable by flood, the earthworks built up under the pretty towers and the natural defence of the river. As the tide flowed from the Seine into the Lézarde it covered the tips of the sharp stakes with which the moat had been sown, ready to rip the bottom from any boat.

Outside Harfleur, Henry celebrated the feast of the Assumption, and his chaplains said the daily offices.

Four days after the landing, Henry sent a party of foot-soldiers and cavalry to surround Harfleur on the eastern side. His brother Thomas, Duke of Clarence led the expedition, making the necessary detour to circumnavigate the flooded paths through the marsh. The August sun was becoming fiercer daily, and the swamp stank foully. Countless stinging insects swarmed in a poisonous cloud about the heads of the men. Crossing a half-drowned ford on his way round behind Harfleur, Clarence felt queasy. His discomfort may have been temporarily dispelled by the seizure of a party of French driving wagonloads of armaments. These had been sent in haste from Rouen by Marshal Jean Boucicaut to aid Harfleur's defences. Now further guns, casks of powder and sheaves of arrows were in English hands, and Clarence established his party east of the town.

While spies slipped nightly out of Harfleur through the darkness and rode to Paris and Rouen with news, the English went about setting up their siege-engines round the seemingly invincible town. As they worked they were threatened constantly by soldiers from the garrison who aimed weapons through the numerous slits in the high towers and the wall. Labourers and gunners struggled in the blistering sun digging gun emplacements and positioning the King's Daughter, the Messenger and the London. Their only defence while working was a movable screen of hinged planks which could be raised and lowered for the guns to be fired.

As Clarence had been riding to gain his easterly position, reinforcements, only just in time, had entered Harfleur. The Sire de Gaucourt had come from Paris at the order of King Charles, bringing a further 300 men-at-arms. Now all these forces loosed a fierce salvo upon the sweating carpenters and gunners below the wall. Crossbow-quarrels thudded into the screens, the mouths of cannon leered smoking from every embrasure, discharging a hail of shot.

Henry had already put his miners to work under the command of Sir John Greyndon. They dug furiously at trenches and tunnels wherever a dry spot allowed, seeking to under-

The English set up their siege engines round the
seemingly invincible town.

mine the base of the town wall. They planted explosives and
ran back from the subterranean roar and rush of falling earth.
The manœuvre was not a total success; the French were coun-
termining to fight in the tunnels and further, were coming
out of the garrison gate in sporadic lunatic sallies, covered by
a hail of shot from the towers and firing as they ran. Behind
a hastily built palisade of wattle and iron, Sir Thomas Erpingham's archers answered – aiming at a few running Frenchmen
who seized luckless artisans from their work and haled them
back into Harfleur.

The great machines were set up at last. The Messenger
spoke, and sent a ball, so large that it needed ten men to load
it and ten to prime the cannon, hurtling towards the bulwarks

of the towers. The thunderous roar knocked the gunners backwards. Flame and black smoke cleared to reveal a satisfying hole in the town wall. The satisfaction was brief; immediately soldiers and citizens rushed to mend the gap, efficiently shoring it up with timber and boulders. The archers fired from behind their palisade, but the garrison from their good vantage point fired back, killing a score of bowmen with missiles from crossbow, veuglaire and crapaudin. The English retaliated savagely, leaping, firing, running for cover, sweating in the choking humid heat filled with gunsmoke and the foulness from the marsh.

Day and night the great guns roared. Balls as big as millstones crashed deafeningly into the wall. Sleep became a thing of memory for besieged and besiegers alike. Life was a constant cannon-roar, an orchestration of whirring arrow-flights and intermittent screams as men died spitted by steel or crushed by stone. At night, both sides lighted their missiles, wrapping pitch-soaked tow round arrows and shot. Parabolas of fire crossed and criss-crossed the moat. Part of the barbican blazed briefly before being extinguished. One of the great guns broke down and the more archaic weapons were swiftly brought into use – the arblasts and mangonels and trebuchets, all catapulting hundreds of pounds of shot at the town walls. If any English troop brought its mobile ladder, a siege-engine called a 'sow', near enough to assault the walls, vats of sulphur and boiling fat were tipped over the men's heads.

For many days the English concentrated their fire on the barbican outside the Leure gate; it was battered and burned as fiery stones weighing five hundred pounds were hurled at it. Sir John Holland was in command of the operation, urging the smoke-blackened, red-eyed, sleepless men. They responded grimly and the barbican began to weaken and crumble. But the siege was already eight days old and there was another enemy now to contend with: the worst enemy of all, as deadly as the stones and crossbow-quarrels of the French. The little queasiness felt by the Duke of Clarence had touched other bellies; dysentery broke out and raged like a famished beast.

Soon after landing off the Chef de Caux, many of the men had wandered off towards the reeking marsh, wading through flood-water to find deserted cottages and farms. The wine-harvest had just begun, and there were gallons of sour new wine to be gulped down before the King could see and reprimand. There were trees and vines heavy with indigestible green grapes and apples, all plunder and therefore seized; and, worst of all, there was the swamp filled with cockles and mussels – irresistible delicacies. The men had gobbled them down. The product of the muddy creeks, they were as lethal as arsenic. The places where they proliferated were the repositories of ordure from the town, and the marsh was a poison-pit. As the epidemic began, men squatted groaning from the bloody flux. Even those who had been abstemious caught the disease, as the miasma from the marsh, midden and fly-infested latrines seemed to soak into their vitals and the filthy insects sucked their blood. By the fourteenth day of the siege the surgeons' tents were bursting with soldiers dying in agony. Even the King's own doctors, Thomas Morestede and William Bradwardyn, were called in to help. Morestede was quickly summoned back to attend the King's brother, Clarence, who was desperately ill, while Bradwardyn rushed to succour the Earls of March and Arundel and Suffolk. Suffolk was dying. And so was the King's dearest friend, Richard Courtenay, Bishop of Norwich.

Henry wept as he closed the Bishop's eyes and washed his feet in a gesture of humility. He had done all he could for his friend, having sent to the English town of Bordeaux for fresh beef and wine and grain, some of which supplies had been captured by French peasants, and he had sent fishermen to catch good eels and pike and sturgeon along the Normandy coast; but rations were growing low and the sickness raged. The Duke of Clarence was by this time so ill that he was sent back to England, fevered, griped by the bloody flux but still conscious enough to swear with disappointment. His humili-

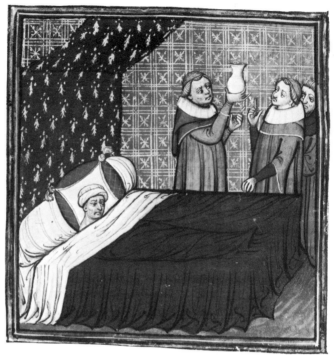

*Many were desperately ill, including the Duke of
Clarence, Henry's brother.
The Earl of Suffolk was one of those who died.*

ating return was a memory that was to rankle with him for
years.

Michael de la Pole, Earl of Suffolk, died in an agony of
blood and waste, and his earldom passed to his young son,
Michael. In the crowded surgeons' tents the doctors worked
ceaselessly and in most cases hopelessly. Bodies of troops, un-
touched by arrow or gunstone, lay stiffening. No herbs,
bleeding or prayers could stop the awful process. Within the
tents the stench was hellish and the nights of roaring guns and
whistling fiery missiles were made heavier by the groans of
dying men.

The Sire d'Estouteville had sent an impertinent message to
King Henry in response to Chester Herald's diplomatic
mission into the town. At the commencement of the siege,

when Henry had the town completely surrounded by Clarence in the east, Suffolk in the west and himself to the north, he had demanded Harfleur's surrender, saying that all Normandy was his by right and in particular this port, which should be handed back by its guards. The garrison commander had promptly replied: '*Vous ne nous avez rien donné à garder, nous n'avons rien à vous rendre.*' ('You have given us nothing to guard, and we have nothing to yield.')

With Suffolk dead and Clarence out of action, other commanders kept the siege-points covered round the town while Sir John Holland's gunners battered the Leure barbican, but an air of desperation began to infiltrate the English army. The heat and humidity worsened. It was torture to move about in armour. Sweat dripped down the sides of even the lightly clad bowmen. The men were dirty, exhausted and despondent, their skins grimed with war-smoke, their nostrils filled with the vile clammy swamp and the corrupting death-smell all around. They were hungry; fewer provisions were getting through from Bordeaux as Marshal Boucicaut, at Rouen, sent ambush parties to block the way. Lack of sleep brought them near to madness. Daily the death-roll grew. Daily the gunstones and burning arrows flew against the walls and barbican, while the townspeople and soldiers continued to mend the damage. And yet, though it is doubtful whether Henry knew this, Harfleur had its calamities too. Besieged thus, their rations were growing low, and there was dysentery within the town also.

Thomas, Earl of Arundel grew weaker and was advised to take ship for home like Clarence, but he refused. With priests and doctors round him, he lay in his gold-latched pavilion and listened to the interminable sounds of siege. Sir John Holland pushed his gunners almost beyond the brink of endurance. Henry, seemingly regardless of hazard, made excursions down to the siege lines and gun emplacements to encourage the men. Looking up, he saw how constant bombardment had destroyed the blue and gold figures on top of the towers. The barbican was in a state of imminent collapse.

Yet he was not cheered and hid his depression with difficulty; the siege had taken far longer than he had envisaged. Soon after the beginning he had sent a message to the English captains at Bordeaux prophesying that Harfleur would be his within eight days; it was now September 16, his twenty-eighth birthday. His challenge to the Dauphin, sent this day and given below, illustrates however that his resolve remained adamantine.

Henry by the grace of God King of England and of France, and Lord of Ireland, to the high and puissant Prince, the Dauphin of Vienne, our Cousin, eldest son of the most puissant Prince, our Cousin and Adversary of France. From the reverence of God, and to avoid the effusion of human blood, We have many times, and in many ways, sought peace, and notwithstanding that We have not been able to attain it, our desire to possess it increases more and more. And well considering that the effect of our wars are the deaths of men, destruction of countries, lamentations of women and children, and so many general evils that every good Christian must lament it and have pity, and We especially, whom this matter more concerns, We are induced to seek diligently for all possible means to avoid the above-mentioned evils, and to acquire the approbation of God, and the praise of the world.

Whereas We have considered and reflected, that as it hath pleased God to visit our said Cousin your Father, with infirmity, with Us and You lie the remedy, and to the end that every one may know that We do not prevent it, We offer to place our quarrel, at the will of God, between Our Person and Yours. And if it should appear to you that you cannot accept this offer on account of the interest which you think our said Cousin your Father has in it, We declare to you that if you are willing to accept it and to do what we propose, it pleases us to permit that our said Cousin, from the reverence of God and that he is a sacred person, shall enjoy that which he at present has for the term of his life, whatever it may please God shall happen between Us and You, as it shall be agreed between his council, ours and yours. Thus, if God shall give us the victory, the crown of France with its appurtenances as our right, shall be immediately rendered to us without difficulty, after his decease, and that to this all the lords and estates of the kingdom of France shall be bound in manner as shall be agreed between us. For it is better for us, Cousin, to decide this war for ever between our two persons, than to suffer the unbelievers by means of our quarrels to destroy Christianity, our mother the Holy Church to remain in division, and the people of God to destroy one another. We pray that you may have such anxious desire to it, and to seek for peace, that you will neglect no means by which it can be obtained. Let us hope in God that a better or shorter way of effecting it cannot be found; and therefore in discharge of our soul, and in charge of yours, if great evils follow, we propose to you what is above said.

Protesting that we make this our offer to the honour and fear of God, and for the reasons above mentioned, of our own motion without our loyal relations, counsellors, and subjects now around us, having in so high a matter dared to advise us; nor can it at any time to come be urged to our prejudice, nor in prejudice of our good right and title which We have at present to the said crown with its appurtenances; nor to the good right and title which We now have to other lands and heritages on this side the sea; nor to our heirs and successors, if this our offer does not take full effect between Us and You, in the manner above said. Given under our Privy Seal, at our town of Harfleur, the xvi day of September.

The challenge remained unanswered.

Grudgingly Henry admired the tenacity with which the citizens fought back, repairing their defences. Hopefully he watched Holland's forces attack the barbican again and again. There were gaps in the town wall through which the citizens could be seen running about like the inhabitants of a kicked antheap. From time to time squadrons of armed men burst suddenly from the garrison and rushed across to the English gun emplacements. They hurled incendiaries – part of the archers' protective palisade sprang into a blaze and several provision wagons exploded as casks of powder caught fire. Clods of earth, steel fragments and burning timbers fell in a rain over the reeling men.

These encouraging little sallies might have put heart into the garrison but for the deeply disturbing knowledge that Harfleur had been virtually deserted by those on whose behalf they laboured to hold it. It was two weeks since a messenger had slipped by night through the English lines to

Vernon where the Dauphin Louis now lay. Reinforcements had been promised, but none had arrived. As the sickness and hunger reached its limit within and without Harfleur, Sir John Holland launched a desperately renewed attack on the Leure gate. Sir John Greyndon's miners dug like frantic moles. Swiftly men threw rafts of timber across the stake-filled moat. The four Dutch master gunners roared commands and the great guns bellowed and spewed millstones at the wall.

Realization that the Dauphin had abandoned it took the heart from the town. Citizens and garrison were as tired, sick and hungry as their besiegers; they limped about among masses of rubble trying to bury their dead and tend their wounded. Half the fine church of St Martin was a smoking ruin. The Sires de Gaucourt and d'Estouteville knew a grim hopelessness. Buildings lay shattered and falling masonry shook the cobbled streets by the minute. And now the barbican was down at last. The English guns were being dragged close to the town walls; siege-ladders arose, battering-rams pounded, men struck wearily and desperately at one another on the battlements. Once more Henry formally demanded the surrender of the town. He was indignant at the loss of time and life during these weeks of filth, hazard and privation and to the Sire de Gaucourt his terms seemed unnecessarily harsh. Once more Chester Herald galloped back over the drawbridge with a defiant reply from the French.

In answer Henry launched the fiercest bombardment of all. With every weapon at his disposal he stormed the town, blowing the fractured wall to pieces and exploding underground charges as if to hurl Harfleur from the face of the earth. Erpingham's archers loosed a rain of fire from their diminished stock of arrows over the palisade and through the wounded wall; in the east the commanders echoed the assault with stones from their huge catapults, while even the sailors from the fleet joined men-at-arms running on makeshift bridges across the moat. For a further twenty-four hours the storm continued until the streets of Harfleur were knee-deep

Heralds go forward to negotiate a truce.

in broken houses and dead men. As dawn broke, a messenger came out to parley with the Earl of Dorset, Sir Thomas Erpingham and Lord Fitzhugh. Still hoping vainly for reinforcements from the Dauphin, the garrison suggested a truce of two weeks.

Henry would have none of it. He had lost over two thousand men, mostly from dysentery, and his supplies were virtually exhausted. His magnificent fighting machine was sadly depleted and he demanded unconditional surrender. Knights like Clarence and March had been sent home to die or recover, while the dying Arundel stayed on in his tent, grimly giving advice. The siege had cost Henry dearly, yet the stubborn citizens still asked for terms. Five days was what they now begged for, so that a deputation led by the Sire de Hacqueville could ride to Vernon and ask the Dauphin again for assistance. With reluctant chivalry Henry agreed, taking twenty-four hostages from the town as surety. For the first time in weeks the sound of gunfire died away.

While Bishop Benedict Nichols celebrated Mass under the smouldering town bastion, accompanied by over sixty clerics and esquires bearing the Eucharist on which both parties had sworn to honour the truce, Henry was secretly confident. Whatever agents he had been able to send towards Vernon and Rouen had verified that the Burgundy–Armagnac feud, so vital to his own success, still festered. Jean sans Peur had made a laconic offer of reinforcements to the Dauphin, which he, dreading reprisals from the Armagnacs, had refused. Through the shortening September days the people of Harfleur looked longingly towards the horizon for a gleam of banners. The horizon remained empty.

King Charles, still more or less in possession of his faculties, had taken the red silk banner of St Denis, the sacred oriflamme, from the cathedral in Paris and had marched with it to Mantes. In reply to a letter received earlier from Henry, he had stated unequivocally:

As none of your predecessors ever had any right, and you still less, to make the demands contained in certain of your letters presented to us by Chester your Herald, nor to cause us any trouble, it is our intention with the assistance of the Lord, in whom we have singular trust . . . to resist you in a way which shall be to the honour and glory of us and of our Kingdom, and to the confusion, loss and dishonour of you and your party.

For all this, he was still unable to mend the strife in his realm sufficiently to gather the troops necessary to give weight to his intention. Heavy taxes bought weapons in plenty, but so far many lords disdained to use them for fear of allying themselves, even against an invader, with a cousinly foe.

The five days were done. Bishop Nichols assured the people of Harfleur that they would be well treated. Were they not, after all, King Henry's subjects? Meanwhile, on the opposite bank of the Seine estuary at Honfleur, Jean Boucicaut, Marshal of France, had arrived from Rouen with a large force, quietly and efficiently gathered. He, unlike many, was alarmed for his country's safety; a responsible officer, he had little time for personal squabbles. Likewise, at Rouen, Constable Charles d'Albret was assembling troops and sending

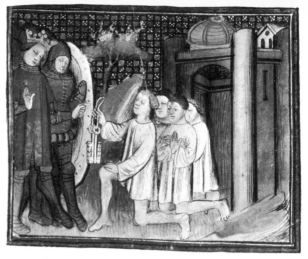

The surrender of Harfleur recalled that of Calais.

spies to determine Henry's next move after the now inevitable surrender of Harfleur.

As Henry had anticipated, the Sire de Hacqueville returned disappointed from Vernon, where there was an impasse. Jean sans Peur (perhaps still hopeful of an alliance with the English against his enemy, Armagnac) had reneged on recent promises made to support the King and Dauphin. It was rumoured that he was only waiting for all troops to be withdrawn from Paris to combat the invasion, to enter the city himself in triumph. He had even imprisoned his own son, Philip, Count of Charolais, who was longing to join battle, at St Omer in the Castle of Aire, and Philip was bitterly disappointed. Nearly all the lords under Jean sans Peur's dominion refused to serve King or Dauphin without their Duke's permission. The Armagnacs were equally unco-operative; although Charles of Orléans promised to send 500 men to Vernon, the Dukes of Bourbon and Berry (chief members of the Orléanist party) withheld their support. When an Armagnac knight was appointed Captain of Picardy, the Burgundians refused to recognize his authority. And so in face of this stalemate, Harfleur fell into English hands on Sunday, 22 September, when the terms of the truce had to be fulfilled.

Henry's bitterness is illustrated in the poetic revenge he imposed on 'his' subjects. He recalled the action of his great-

Henry V's battle helm dented at Agincourt.

grandfather, Edward III, after the gruelling siege of Calais nearly seventy years earlier, when the burgesses had been forced into the royal presence with ropes round their necks. It was a humiliation he saw fitting to repeat. The Sires Raoul de Gaucourt and Lionel de Bracquemont, together with several other aristocrats and the twenty-four hostages, were commanded to wear hair shirts, 'shirts of penitence' and felons' halters, and so were conducted into the English camp. They were forced to kneel for long periods in the tent of lord after lord until they came to where Henry, sumptuously dressed and sitting in a gold pavilion, awaited delivery of the keys of the town. He kept the hostages on their knees for a further half-hour, looking loftily and silently over their heads. Sir Gilbert Umfraville stood at his right, holding a pikestaff bearing Henry's tilting helm surmounted by the crown of England. All the principal lords and officers watched until the long ritual was complete, then Henry motioned to Thomas Beaufort, Earl of Dorset, to take the keys.

He then spoke at length to the French knights. He accused them of withholding his town in defiance of God and justice. Yet: 'as they had given themselves up to his mercy, he would not be merciless.' From the last of the hoarded rations from Bordeaux he gave them supper. His impressive retinue waited on them in as leisurely and courtly a manner as if at home in the Palace of Westminster. The knights filled bellies shrunken by the siege, while Henry, fasting in private thanks-giving, apprised all those present of his plans for Harfleur.

The pretty little ruined town was to be rebuilt and become an English port and garrison, just as Calais was. The masons and craftsmen whom he had brought from home would set to work directly to repair the siege-damage, and all able-bodied citizens were welcome to stay and help, provided they took the oath of allegiance. Wealthy men were en-couraged to ransom themselves; to Henry, funds were a necessity if his campaign were to continue. The Sires de

The pretty little ruined town was rebuilt.

Gaucourt, d'Estouteville, de Hacqueville and all other prominent knights were allowed parole to raise their ransoms
and present these at Calais on November 11. In London and
other large English towns proclamations would be made of
the capture of Harfleur and merchants and tradespeople en-
couraged to emigrate and continue their living by grants of
houses and privilege. A degree of plunder was of course inevitable, all movables being forfeit to the army and their
commanders, and the prime valuables would be taken aboard
the *Trinité Royale*, while Henry decreed a complete inventory
of the citizens' possessions. Humphrey, Duke of Gloucester
was to oversee this, with freedom to hang anyone making a
false declaration, a measure that was not, in the event, en-
forced. Harfleur, Henry said confidently, would soon regain
its old prosperity.

This Utopian prospect, with everyone working in amiable
harness under the English Governor, a post now given to
Henry's uncle, Thomas Beaufort, Earl of Dorset, was marred
by what today would be considered an inhuman act. Then,
however, it was mere expediency: Henry realized that if
Harfleur were to survive as a frontier town subject to constant siege there would be no room for stragglers. He therefore ordered the crippled, the aged and the infirm to leave
immediately, ordaining that five sous apiece should be given
to speed their passage. The following morning 2000 departed
in a pathetic, weeping file, the maimed and blind, girls with
ancient fathers and young babies, the sick being carried on
rafts of wood. They passed under the gate where the King's
standard and the banner of St George were whipping in the
autumn wind. Expediency was a word rooted in the mind of
all medieval kings and in Henry's as firmly as the belief that
his cause, after all, was God's.

While the sad procession passed, he entered the battered
shell of St Martin's church and prayed barefoot for several
hours before calling a council meeting. Harfleur was won,
but his inheritance, the greatness he had promised himself,
was still as nebulous as a mirage. It was time to plan again.

And taking many a fort,
Furnished in warlike sort,
Marcheth tow'rds Agincourt
    In happy hour;
Skirmishing day by day
With those that stopp'd his way.
Where the French general lay
    With all his power.

MICHAEL DRAYTON: *Agincourt*

The March

The taint of the usurper's son still lingered painfully in Henry's mind as he surveyed the councillors now awaiting his decision. The words of the Archbishop of Bourges – 'You have no right!' – still stung. He had embarked on this enterprise in the hope of a tangible glory evidenced in captured lands and towns. By now, the beginning of October, he should have achieved something to justify, in England, not only the heavy financial outlay but also his own position, so that his sovereignty could never again be disputed.

With dismay he reviewed the outcome of these gruelling weeks in France. One small harbour town was his where by now he should be in control of provinces. Even as his masons and carpenters began the rebuilding of Harfleur he knew with appalling certainty that the prospect of further conquest was slim. Of the 9000 men he had brought from England, at least 2000 were dead, the majority from sickness, including at least 1500 of the priceless archers. One of the dead was Henry's friend Sir John Philip. His tomb in St Mary's, Kidderminster, records their friendship, says he fought well at Harfleur, and died on 2 October. Moreover, men who had survived the dysentery were debilitated and downcast. Two ships, the *Catherine* and the *Holy Ghost* from Winchelsea, had lately anchored laden with provisions for the rebuilding which included rope, glue, coal and grain. Now they took aboard more sick troops destined for home. A thousand further men

An army on the march.

could be discounted; whatever course was next decided upon, these must stay to garrison Harfleur.

Henry had planned originally to march from Harfleur along the Seine valley, enter Rouen and Paris and then go south-west in triumph to Bordeaux, a distance of some 350 miles. Now, as the surgeons brought their dreadful daily bulletins, he recognized the impossibility of his scheme. With him were now little over half the fighting force which had set out two months earlier. Winter was approaching, the weather sharpening. Rations were once more alarmingly low. The trees were shedding their leaves; for miles around the fields were bare. Anyone but Henry would have been tempted to return home, borrow more money, gather fresh forces and set out again next summer to complete the campaign. But by then the first burning inspiration would have been lost for ever, the curse of the usurper's son would be whispered, and God's cause would be mocked. To abandon the enterprise now was unthinkable. Even with the decimated, demoralized force, the watchwords were still prowess and glory – glory or death.

He had with him a mere 900 men-at-arms and 5000 archers. Yet his mind was set. At the War Council he announced that the army should go forward to Calais; a chevauchée on which they would do battle with any army seeking to block their path and during which they would take what gains they might. The chevauchée, literally meaning 'a ride', had become a popular feature of military strategy and involved much pillaging en route, meanwhile provoking the enemy into offering battle or at least weakening his resistance and resources should no battle be offered. Once at Calais, the army could be re-victualled and perhaps gather reinforcements from the Earl of Warwick's garrison there.

The councillors were appalled at his temerity. It had been established that Charles d'Albret had a growing force at Rouen, near which such a chevauchée would need to pass. South-east was the Dauphin, at Vernon, and he was capable of moving as soon as the army left its entrenched position at

Harfleur. The dying Earl of Arundel pointed out the additional threat of Jean sans Peur of Burgundy, who could summon a magnificent force to King Charles's aid if he so wished, and whose equivocal attitude could resolve itself at any moment.

And yet, sitting in the Council pavilion near the poisonous marsh, hearing the grave-diggers' spades, Henry was adamant, prepared for risk and hazard. He was willing to march with his frail army and dwindling supplies through unknown territory. On the opposite bank of the estuary at Honfleur, the camp fires of Marshal Boucicaut's army could be seen; this in itself was a spur, yet not half so keen as the reckless resolution burning in Henry. It was an insanity of glory, underlined by the constant belief that the cause was God's. Now they must march fast, slip past d'Albret's force at Rouen and be across the Somme, the greatest obstacle but the river nearest to Calais, before the Dauphin's troops at Vernon could join d'Albret's in a pincer movement and cut them off. He told his Council:

I am possessed with a burning desire to see my territories and the places which ought to be my inheritance. Even if our enemies enlist the greatest armies, my trust is in God, and they shall not hurt my army nor myself. I will not allow them, puffed up with pride, to rejoice in misdeeds, nor unjustly, against God, to possess my goods. They would say that through fear I have fled away acknowledging the injustice of my cause. But I have a mind, my brave men, to encounter all dangers, rather than let them brand your King with word of ill-will. With the favour of God we will go unhurt and inviolate, and if they attempt to stop us, victorious and triumphant in all glory.

He issued final orders. Apart from Dorset, who was to stay as governor of Harfleur, Sir Thomas Erpingham, Sir Gilbert Umfraville, Edward, Duke of York, Sir John Cornwall and Sir John Holland and all the other commanders were to make ready. The chevauchée would move off at dawn.

The army was relieved to be quitting the noxious graveyard of Harfleur, but the sun had departed and white mist lapped the horses' hooves to the pasterns as the columns rolled forward in the October morning. As speed was paramount, the army travelled light, with provisions for only eight days. Henry planned to march at the rate of seventeen miles per day, a rate determined by the foot-soldiers and wagons. Even he was unsure of the distance (160 miles) to Calais, judging it less than it really was. The route too was uncertain, and the only available maps must have been crude and obscure. There was need to rely on the childhood memories of old knights such as Thomas Erpingham, who recalled the route taken by Edward III on his way to triumph at Crécy. There were two rivers to be crossed before the Somme – the Béthune and the Bresle – and several small towns to pass during these crossings, among them Fécamp, Arques, and Boves.

The best place to ford the Somme appeared to be a tidal cattle-ford five miles downstream from Abbeville named the White Spot (Blanche-Tâque), over which Edward III's army had moved in a formation of twelve abreast. It must have crossed the minds of the commanders that Edward's army had been vastly different from the one now setting out: a well-provisioned, well-fed army, healthy and strong, whereas the men now loading the pack-animals with their gear looked pitiful. They were grim-faced from hunger and siege, their jacques and gloves and shoes of boiled leather already rotting from the damp, their wounds only half-healed, their helmets battered. The lords' plate armour was stowed on the backs of the sumpter-horses and as many weapons as could be carried at speed were piled into carts. The three great guns which had broken into Harfleur were of necessity left behind at the garrison. The chevauchée was a desperate gamble.

Hours before the march began, Henry sent a team of fast couriers ahead to Calais telling the Earl of Warwick to expect him and, more important, to send a decoy contingent of troops to engage any force of d'Albret's that might come south of the Somme to block the army's path. Everything depended on an unhindered fording of Blanche-Tâque, and all was speculation: whether Burgundy would suddenly move either to help King Charles or, contrarily, the English

Many civilians were forced to leave Harfleur.

invader; whether the French would submit to watching this small impudent force march unmolested through upper Normandy; whether that force could outmarch any opposition spearheaded from Rouen.

Henry's holy relics and vessels were carefully loaded into his personal baggage-wagon. His piece of the True Cross was being respectfully guarded by a Sergeant of the Pantry. The chaplains celebrated Mass and then prepared to march with the rest, while the King addressed his army, reiterating the edicts against pillage and rape and despoilment of the Church. Then they moved forward, heading north towards Montivilliers in the traditional formation of three main bodies with two columns of flank-guards walking or riding to left and right.

Commanding the vanguard were Sir John Cornwall and Sir Gilbert Umfraville. Behind in the main body rode Henry and his brother Humphrey of Gloucester, Lord de Roos and Sir John Holland, the new Earl of Huntingdon, to whom Henry had restored the family honours for his prowess during the siege. Rearward came Edward, Duke of York and Richard de Vere, Earl of Oxford. The wagons trundled along between the columns and the archers trudged at the flanks, carrying their longbows slung on their shoulders. Banners and pennons drooped dispiritedly in the cold October morning. The iron cartwheels crackled on the beginnings of frost. The quartermasters had issued each man with a small loaf of stale bread, a hunk of dried salt beef or pork, a flask of watered wine, and men who had only half-recovered from sickness found these iron rations nauseating fare. It is possible that on that first day's march the army encountered a homeless knot of refugees from Harfleur – the old and maimed, women with babies, all weeping with hunger. The pittance of five sous allocated to each by Henry had already been stolen by the bandits with which the open country of Normandy abounded.

The army marched towards Fécamp through fields already harvested and past vineyards stripped of their yield. The countryside was sparsely populated although a few frightened faces peeped from cottage windows as the columns moved doggedly on and frost gave way to mud along roads pitted with holes and strewn with rocks likely to lame animals and men alike. News of the advance, probably through the spies of Marshal Boucicaut, had already reached Fécamp. Under the Captain of Boulogne a small army awaited them, an army which in the three or four days at Fécamp had behaved more like an invading than a defending force, looting the town and ravishing the women. As the English reached the walls of the town, an armed contingent galloped out. A detachment of flank-guards composed of archers and men-at-arms closed in battle with it, and there was a short, hot little skirmish. Some hand-to-hand fighting took place, the English forcing a little way into the town, and there were minor losses on both sides. The encounter was soon over, but when Henry's army passed by, the Abbey of Fécamp was ablaze. It is uncertain whether French or English had started the fire. Although the French soldiers were uncomfortable guests for Fécamp to entertain, there is little doubt that Henry's army did not behave in the puritan manner he had advocated or as English chroniclers suggest. In fact, a Parisian writing later about the chevauchée states that great depredations were made on the countryside by English and French alike.

had heard of the surrender and sack of Harfleur, was badly frightened. His willingness to see the army safely on its way extended to re-victualling it with twenty wagonloads of fresh bread – an unexpected bonus for the hungry men.

Encouraged as much as it could be (there were still sick and suffering in the train), the army moved on. Meanwhile a French council at Rouen was discussing the chevauchée and deciding upon future strategy. Agents of Boucicaut and d'Albret had brought news that the English force was weak, ill and under strength. A recommendation was put forward that these puny troops should be allowed to gain Calais and return to England while every effort was made to regain Harfleur. The Constable and the Marshal of France were in favour of this, but more impetuous commanders such as the Duke of Bourbon and the old Duke of Berry, veteran of Poitiers, rebelled. Although such a small bedraggled army was scarcely worth a fight, it could not be allowed to pass unchallenged. A heated pride arose in the French noblemen. The prospect of wiping out Henry's army was held as such a *fait accompli* that when word spread and various towns offered a contingent of armed forces these were disdainfully referred to as 'unnecessary little merchants' and accepted with arrogance and ill-will. Slowly, gradually, the hereditary aristocrats of France began to band together, grudging their mutual bondage yet anxious to rid the realm of this unworthy foe.

The march continued, shrouded in mist-fine rain. Feet sank deeper into mud and nearly every evening the rain came on harder. The commanders, at Henry's bidding, ordered the pace quickened and sleep became rationed as well as food. By night tents were raised for the nobles, the lesser ranks spread straw for themselves, and the lowest wedged themselves into ditches under leafless hedges or in the forks of trees. The horses' legs were splashed to the hock with mire. The lords' armour ran with damp and patches of rust began to show. The bowmens' leather gloves and footwear rotted further and were abandoned on the broken roads. The little Irishmen were clothed only in mud. The horses grew thin and tired, existing on mouthfuls of snatched sparse grass. The 6000 men were lean and scarred and weary, their teeth loosened by the bad diet, the scanty slivers of leathery salt meat and the brackish water. Soon the bread ration from Arques was finished. Home seemed very far away, and Calais just as far.

A rate of some twenty miles a day found them soon at the second river, the Bresle, and embroiled in an outbreak of fighting east of the town of Eu, between Dieppe and Abbeville. Cannon fired from the walls and a few men were lost. Undaunted, Henry sounded trumpets and advanced banners, striking out with his foot-soldiers and archers and, as at Arques, lighting torches as a gesture of threat. To the lonely little stone town standing amid desolate October fields, the army, thin and threadbare as it was, looked none the less menacing. Fearing fire, the town capitulated, waving the army on across the river and once more augmenting Henry's pantry and buttery with rations. The men's spirits rose a trifle. As they billeted themselves in the damp open country across the Bresle, the word 'Calais' took on a less nebulous aspect.

As appears to have been his custom on almost every evening, Henry walked among the troops, dressed in common garb and spreading the occasional word of encouragement. He kept in close contact with his men as well as his officers; he knew their fatigue, admired their doggedness on the march. There had been very few deserters, and discipline was good. Nightly he tried to offer them words of cheer, although he was as weary as they.

He believed that the road to Calais still lay open and that any force trying to block his passage would have been dealt with by the decoy guard he had summoned from Calais. He had little idea at this time that in Rouen the discussions and arguments had ceased and that the muster of men had begun.

Henry kept in close contact with his men as well
as his officers.

At long last a sense of national emergency seemed to have awakened. The Dauphin Louis received a large contingent of knights and men-at-arms, most of them naturally of the Armagnac party. The Dukes of Alençon and Bar joined Bourbon and Berry, and King Louis of Sicily, who was the second Duke of Anjou and cousin to King Charles, arrived with a big force. The Duke of Brittany, who had earlier refused to serve, now promised 12,000 men, and the Count of Richemont came with 500 lancers. The young Charles, Duke of Orléans brought his crack fighting force, while the Count of Nevers and Antoine, Duke of Brabant, brothers of Jean sans Peur, agreed to uphold the Crown. Jean sans Peur himself remained as usual uncommitted. The citizens of Paris offered 6000 well-armed men. In all, the muster at Rouen yielded some 60,000 men, among them 15,000 men-at-arms. There were thousands of crossbowmen, and countless mercenaries of all nationalities, anxious to do their share of pillaging after what looked like an inevitable victory. Henry's army was outmatched by ten to one.

The French dukes and counts polished their massive plate armour and groomed their beautiful horses until their coats shone like glass. Now that they were committed to do battle with this despised little army, each nobleman sought especial glory. Every French knight put on his brightest colours, trying to outdo his neighbour. The feuds, although at the moment quiescent, were far from forgotten. The knights were still as arrogant and contemptuous of one another as they were of Henry's army. They swelled with pride, growing more excitable and tense and intemperately glorious as the days passed, as the rain and mist deepened, and as Henry learned to his disquiet that the road to Calais was far from clear.

A few miles from the Somme and the coveted ford of Blanche-Tâque, a solitary prisoner fell into English hands. A Gascon mercenary, he told the King he was one of the soldiers under the command of Constable d'Albret. He could well have been planted solely to undermine the English morale, for the news he gave Henry was so alarming that at

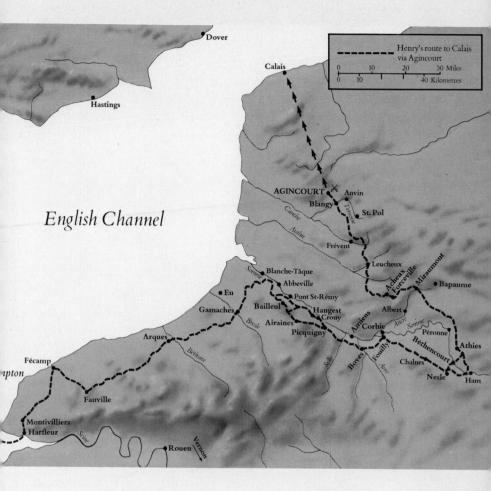

Henry's route from Harfleur to Calais via Agincourt.

first he was disbelieved, Gascons being by tradition given to exaggeration. In this instance, he spoke the disastrous truth, demanded by Henry on pain of beheading. The advance guard sent for from Calais and intended to keep Blanche-Tâque open, had been outmarched. Constable d'Albret, commanding the vanguard of the French army, had moved east from Abbeville to march parallel with the chevauchée. Even now an unseen great force kept step with Henry's weary train. Marshal Boucicaut, whom all had thought to be a hundred miles south at Honfleur, had marched even faster than the English. Now, his guard of 6000 men kept watch at Blanche-Tâque. The river there, as at nearly all other fords, had been filled with stakes, tree-trunks and chains, making a crossing impossible. The English army, said the Gascon, was being watched from the northern bank. It would be driven upstream where the combined forces of d'Albret and Boucicaut would put it to the sword.

When Henry had dismissed the Gascon, the war councillors clustered, full of trepidation. Even Sir Gilbert Umfraville, a brave and experienced soldier, voiced doubts that the march could now succeed, and suggested returning to Harfleur. The King treated this notion with contempt: Sir Gilbert and any others of like mind could return if they wished, but the chevauchée would continue. This reckless decision was forced on Henry; by now nearly the whole of upper Normandy and Picardy were swarming with French armed parties and to turn back would present no less a hazard than to continue. It was of paramount importance that the Somme be crossed soon, and when the tidal ebb was lowest. Once more they went forward, up the valley, passing Amiens, veering southeast past Pont St Rémy and Hangest-sur-Somme, always searching for an unguarded ford. Scouts were sent off and returned with tales of troops lying in wait on the river bank. The army veered further east, passing through Crouy and Picquigny. The landscape seemed deserted but there was the

Boucicaut's army of 6000 kept watch at the ford of
Blanche-Tâque.

dispiriting knowledge of being always under surveillance. Rations were at their lowest. All the dried meat was gone; the tired, apprehensive men snatched hazelnuts and berries from the bushes as they straggled forward over the dirty, broken roads.

Thomas Elmham, writing later, summed up the despair which fell upon the men.

> I who write, and many others raised our bitterly anxious eyes to heaven imploring for the mercy of the Almighty's celestial regard. And we besought the glorious Virgin Mary and the blessed St George, under whose protection the most invincible crown of England had flourished of old, to mediate for us between God and our poor people.

At the little town of Boves they were challenged by the garrison but the castellan (one of Burgundy's adherents and essentially non-belligerent for this reason) agreed to let them stay the night and then pass unmolested. While Henry's heralds were bargaining to this end, some of the soldiers found a hoard of wine left unattended. It was the one bright spot in this miserable march. They began an orgy of drinking, only to be discovered by Henry. Angry and alarmed at this indiscipline, he ordered the wine-casks smashed. When the men begged to be allowed to fill their water-bottles with wine, the answer was brisk. 'Bottles!' Henry cried. 'You have made bottles of your bellies!' Grumbling but still obedient, the army moved on the following day.

They then witnessed another and more serious manifestation of the King's wrath. One of the archers had entered a church in Boves and stolen a pyx containing the Eucharist, concealing the vessel in his ragged sleeve. Henry ordered the culprit to be bound and led through the ranks while the charge of sacrilege was read out for all to hear. God's cause had been defiled. Any such further depredations and the Almighty could well desert the army. The archer was summarily hanged from the branch of an oak, and the men, awed and silent, marched by.

Looters in Henry's army were summarily executed.

Wherever they sought a fording place it was discovered that the bridge had been broken and the river filled with sharp timbers. The tide swelled the Somme and covered these hazards as the chevauchée trudged on, north-easterly now, its route made untidy and looping by the diversions necessary to avoid the bands of armed French lurking between the towns. To confuse the unseen troops keeping step with the army's progress, Henry ordered that every village through which they passed should be burned, the inhabitants first being warned in time to escape. Most villages were quite deserted, however, and even the livestock had been hastily butchered and carted away rather than left to re-victual the invader. A pall of black smoke rose from barren fields and thatches of abandoned cottages. The wary, weary men, existing now almost totally on hazelnuts, roots grubbed from the earth and muddy stream-water, pressed on eight miles north-east, where, at Corbie, they saw for the first time the colours of the enemy.

A large party of armed and mounted knights surged out over the bridge. They flew glorious banners starred with a myriad coloured devices. The azure and gold of the French lily and the blood-red oriflamme of St Denis whipped in a frenzy of speed as the fine tall horses pounded down upon Henry's foot-soldiers. A flank-guard of archers fired long-bows in a desperate attempt to halt the cavalry charge, but the range was too close: most of the arrows sailed harmlessly over the heads of the advance and there was no time to reload. Archers and foot-soldiers were flattened in the mud. It was an ignominious encounter during which one of the French knights tore the standard from the hands of Guienne Herald. John Bromley, Groom of the King's Chamber, fought fiercely and successfully for its repossession. The skirmish raged briefly, the most savage up to now. Henry's army was pushed back to the mouth of the narrow bridge and the French cavalry rode back within the garrison. Henry had hoped desperately to cross the Somme at Corbie, but it was far too well guarded.

He had, however, taken prisoner half a dozen French knights. They were calm and confident of being ransomed, which was indeed Henry's intention. Yet it irked him that his priceless archers should have been rendered so impotent, and he fancied the French had found the incident amusing, like the traditional jest that all Englishmen were born with tails. His mind became deeply exercised with the old problem of archers versus charging cavalry. It was the stout Edward, Duke of York, always anxious to retain the royal favour, who reminded him that there was an answer. At the battle of Nicopolis, where the King's father, Henry Bolingbroke, had fought the Turks in 1396, the Sultan Bayard had first used the *chevaux de frise*. This was a fence of sharpened stakes obliquely placed some yards in front of the contingent of archers so as to impale the horses of the cavalry advance as they gathered speed. Each man was now ordered to cut himself such a stake from the hedges and carry it for the remainder of the march. The tired soldiers grumbled and cursed (doubtless out of earshot of the King) at this extra burden, and it is unlikely that any foresaw the vital part these stakes were to play.

At Fouilly, near Corbie, Henry decided to change direction. Between Amiens and Ham the Somme's course bends to the east towards Péronne. Instead of following this curve he turned southwards for Chaulnes and Nesle, planning to cut across the loop of the river. The French on the north bank would need to cover the triangular territory between Corbie, Péronne and Nesle, but it would be possible to reach a hoped-for crossing before d'Albret's forces could catch up with the army. It was another gamble; desperately the commanders pushed the men on. By now they marched like automata, groaning with hunger, and with Calais still a hundred miles away. They had no idea of their real good fortune. Had there been any proper organization or military foresight among the French who shadowed them, Henry's dream would have been ended days ago. There was a score of points on the march where the little army could have been crushed. As it was, the vast and growing French force waited and prepared and squabbled among themselves. They fixed glowing feathered panaches to their helmets, admired their reflections in burnished plate mail, while Henry with his ragged band pressed on over the chalky terrain. At Nesle, defiant peasants had hung out the oriflamme and Henry, his temper short, threatened to burn homes and crops unless his men could be billeted within the town. He still thought of the French as *his* people, and their obstinacy angered him.

Dismally the people of Nesle agreed to his ultimatum. During the night the soldiers scavenged what food was available and possibly performed in stealth other excesses forbidden by Henry. By now the army had learned discretion, but there were women and wine within the town. It would seem likely that Nesle was anxious to see the backs of the English. In the early hours a party of town elders sought an audience with the war council, and handed it the most valuable information so far. There were two fords as yet unguarded and

Tents pitched beside a river.

unspoiled: one at Béthencourt and another at Voyennes in the north-west. Immediately Henry sent out a reconnaisance party, who returned to confirm that the crossings were clear. Shortly before dawn the army moved off, anxious not to lose what could be the last opportunity to cross the Somme.

The men-at-arms and archers took the northerly road to Voyennes, while the pack-train, under guard, moved off on the lower Béthencourt road. The going grew treacherous and swampy, where the river Ingon ran through a marsh to meet the Somme. Most of the roads were built up into causeways, and the army picked its way slowly along the soggy paths. At Voyennes they found that a guarding force from St Quentin had, before departing, broken up the causeway at its final length. At once the men were set to repairing it. They tore down deserted houses, the carpenters and joiners sawing and hammering at planks and tree-trunks and gates to form a makeshift road across the marsh, while Henry sent word to the officers commanding the wagons down at Béthencourt

An army crossing a river.

to join him. Starting at eight o'clock in the morning, by noon
the work was half-completed. Henry participated fully; as
the engineers laboured he gave advice and rode his horse up
and down the completed sections to test them for safety. He
sent a party of archers across to form a bridgehead on the far
side against any attacking force. In single file they were able
to wade across the ebbing river and by evening the causeway
was capable of bearing the carts. Just before nightfall the last
man waded across. A weary little cheer arose. Frogs sang,
the usual evening drizzle baptized the damp, dogged company. The Somme was gained at last, and as the men billeted
themselves round Athies and Monchy-Lagache, a gleam of
optimism flourished. The troops were almost worked to ex-
haustion, but they were on the right side for Calais.

They would not have been so cheerful had they known
that, six miles northward at Péronne, the armies of France,
mighty and more or less in accord at last, awaited them in
arrogant splendour.

135

They now to fight are gone.
Armour on armour shone,
Drum now to drum did groan,
  To hear was wonder;
That with the cries they make
The very earth did shake:
Trumpet to trumpet spake,
  Thunder to thunder.

MICHAEL DRAYTON: *Agincourt*

But if the cause be not good, the king himself
hath a heavy reckoning to make; when all those legs,
and arms, and heads, chopped off in a battle,
shall join together at the latter day, and cry all –
We died at such a place; some, swearing; some,
crying for a surgeon; some, upon their wives
left poor behind them; some, upon the debts they
owe; some, upon their children rawly left. I am
afeard there are few die well that die in a battle.

SHAKESPEARE: *Henry V*,
Act IV, Sc. 1

The Battle

Although Constable d'Albret and Marshal Boucicaut would still have preferred to employ Fabian tactics, harassing and shadowing Henry's debilitated army until it surrendered from lack of morale, the proud French nobles were now keen to join battle. King Charles and the Dauphin both expressed a wish to lead the assault, but were dissuaded by the King's uncle, the old Duke of Berry, and d'Albret was appointed Commander in Chief. The vanguard was given to Boucicaut and the Duke of Bourbon, d'Albret was to ride in the central body and the rearguard was promised to the Duke of Bar and the Counts of Nevers and Vaudémont. The wings were to be commanded by the Count

Jean Boucicaut praying to St Catherine.

of Richemont and Sir Tanneguy du Châtel, and another great lord, Guillaume Martel, was to bear the oriflamme in battle. These and other knights drew up their battle-plan as they lay at Péronne, and on Sunday, 20 October, three heralds of Duke Charles of Orléans and the Duke of Bourbon rode the few miles to Henry's camp with a formal challenge.

Henry had by now learned from his scouts that his army had passed Amiens just before the French force on 17 October, but that during the day spent repairing the causeway the enemy had spurted forward and outmarched them. When the heralds arrived, the men were snatching some rest; they were dirty, wet, famished, their clothes rotten and their spirits jaded. Henry, very calm, courteously welcomed the French emissaries when they were brought to his pavilion by Edward, Duke of York. They carried bright banners and were splendidly attired in the colours of their lords, well-fed, their horses sleek, their armour polished. They knelt, and one began diplomatically: 'Right puissant Prince, great and noble is thy kingly power, as is reported among our lords.'

They went on to inform him that they knew of his intent to conquer the towns and castles of the realm of France and to depopulate her cities, and that for this reason the greatest lords were assembled to defend their rights and that before he reached Calais they would be avenged of his conduct. Henry remained impassive and replied: 'Be all things according to the will of God.' He then reiterated his determination to march straight to Calais, telling them that if his passage were hindered it would be to the utmost peril of the French. With a confidence that in the circumstances seems incredible, he said: We advise them again not to interrupt our journey, nor to seek what would be its consequence: a great shedding of Christian blood.

There was nothing more to say. Henry paid the heralds for their courtesy as was customary, giving each a hundred gold crowns, and they rode back to Péronne with news of his inflexibility. They had by now seen the pitiful state of his army and were doubtless bewildered by his insouciance. English-

Heralds were customarily paid for their courtesy.

men, they must have thought, were not only born with tails: they were born madmen. On the other hand they may have grudgingly admired Henry's attitude.

His calmness was perhaps not unfounded. If there were now to be a battle he could not have picked a place more advantageous to himself and his army. Péronne lay in a valley before him and the sloping terrain was perfect for the deployment of archers and flanking foot-soldiers even against the great force whose number he still did not know for sure. But unfortunately he had named no arbitrary venue, and all day the troops stared down the hill watching for the movements of the enemy. None occurred. The clammy October evening closed like a dank fist on an empty horizon, leafless trees and a stillness that became ominous with the night. Henry went among his men where they occupied their defensive positions and spoke quietly to small groups of them, bidding them be calm and have courage. When it seemed certain that no attack would take place within the next few hours he told them to rest and make ready to resume the march at dawn.

A cloudburst accompanied their departure. As they passed Péronne and moved into the valley through which ran the little river Cologne, a small force left the town and rode towards the English as if to engage them, but the marching columns went steadily on through the downpour and clinging mud. There was no sign of the host of French who had waited in the valley the previous day. But, about a mile outside Péronne, at a crossroads leading to Albert in the northwest and Bapaume in the north-east, evidence, total and terrifying, was visible of what faced the marchers. In the stew of mud where the road forked were the imprints of a myriad hooves, tens of thousands of mailed feet, deep rainfilled gouges where cannon-wagons had trundled by. The sharp wind blew rain into the men's eyes as they stared in horror at the churned morass, and their spirits dipped. An unimaginable host had passed this point along the Bapaume road to seek a place of battle. It seemed as if all the war-horses in the world and every fighting man ever born had set his mark

upon the mud. Disaster appeared inevitable. Mired from
head to foot, they heard the mourning voices of the chaplains raised in prayer: 'crying for God to have compassion
upon us, and of his infinite goodness to turn away from us
the power of the French.' Too disheartened now even to
swear, the men began to echo the prayers. Their soaked rags
whipped in the storm-rain; they still clutched their weapons
and the stout stakes sharpened at both ends. With the knowledge that death marched close, they squelched and struggled
haggardly on towards Albert through the mud.

They covered sixteen miles that day, with the flank-guards
on the right drawing off a little to cover the territory lying
between the main march and the town of Miraumont. By
22 October they had reached Forceville and Acheux, and a
further eighteen miles brought them to Frévent and the bridge
over another small river, the Canche, swollen with rain. At
Leucheux they had passed the Count of St Pol's château-fort,
but no opposition showed itself from the walls. All the opposition lay ahead, unseen yet a monstrous reality. In the minds
of the filthy, downcast men the memory of those countless
footprints remained, while scouts from the right flank returned to report that many thousands of the enemy, having
maintained their parallel march since Bapaume, were drawing
in closer towards them. Edward, Duke of York sent a reconnaissance party ahead of the army and on 23 October it entered the Ternoise valley and approached the village of Blangy.

As the evening of the 23rd came down, Henry's party lost
itself briefly, as the advance guard appears to have done on a
few previous occasions. The King by-passed by about a mile
and a half the night billet selected by his harbingers. Although
floundering in the wet gloom, he refused to turn back. 'God
would not be pleased if I should turn back now,' he said, 'for
I am wearing my côte d'armes.' By this he meant the cloth
tabard showing his arms and devices which was worn over
armour. Since the crossing of the Somme he and all his officers had been wearing their côtes d'armes, showing themselves emblazoned in their martial colours. In rain and darkness

they pressed on to Frévent. There could be no back-tracking. Again, had the French owned only one great leader such as Henry himself, they could with such a leader's initiative have moved in and crushed the English army at almost any given juncture. But the army now arraying itself in magnificence a few miles ahead had many leaders, too many officers, a mélange of arrogance and pride calculated to spoil any army. Sidelong ambushes were not for them; they were ready now, and determined that the English should see them standing in all their glory. That time was not far off.

On 24 October both armies were across the Ternoise river, Henry crossing at Blangy and the French a few miles north-west at Anvin. Beyond Blangy a sudden ridge rose some 300 feet, cutting off all vision of the fields and road, and it was up this hill that Edward of York sent a scout to survey whatever lay ahead. From where he looked through fine rain he could see three villages, each surrounded by a wood. To the north-west was Agincourt, where a decrepit-looking castle was visible, north-east was Tramecourt, and Maisoncelles lay nearest to the south. Out of sight in the distance was Ruisseau-ville. The area between the woods of Tramecourt and Agin-court narrowed to about three-quarters of a mile, widening slightly towards Maisoncelles in a territory more or less tri-angular which lay directly across the road to Calais. As the scout watched, the massed trees seemed to move and shimmer under rain. Then at last, revealed not as moving trees but merging with the rain-wet boles and branches and coming inexorably into view, was the most daunting sight a man could witness. Pouring across the valley in wave after slow wave through a narrow gap to the right rolled three vast columns of sumptuously armed men.

The immensity of the French force was such that Thomas Elmham likened it to an innumerable horde of locusts. It must have seemed to the scout that the whole world glittered there, packed close, then rolling outwards as far as the eye could see to distant Ruisseauville. The three columns looked limitless, mighty as biblical hosts. Between the woodlands a

Sumptuously armed knights in battle.

gigantic forest of flesh and steel took root, a legendary terror as dense as smoke. Spear-heads glinted; there was lance after lance, standard upon standard, cavalry, crossbowmen, foot-soldiers, and endless rows of weapons, an incalculable number of death-devices such as arblasts, mangonels, bombardes, veuglaires, crapaudins – weapons like those left behind, through necessity, at Harfleur by the English army.

Even from the distant vantage point the vigour of the French was apparent. Not only their vast number but their buoyant health and strength. They were well-fed, wined and provisioned, their massive armour bright, their great horses lively, their côtes d'armes rich with colour, their flesh healthy and their spirits high. There were an overwhelming number of ducal standards; from almost every line countless pennons and bannerets flapped and twinkled as the enormous force slowly filled the valley as far as the woods on either side. They drew up in this position with finality.

It was a strange position in which to take a stand. The trees on either flank were an undoubted encumbrance, but it is unlikely that the terrified scout registered this fact. All he could see was a massive army, at least six and possibly ten times greater than the English. He rode downhill, trembling and breathless, to the Duke of York, saying: 'Quickly, be prepared for battle, as you are just about to fight against a world of innumerable people.'

King Henry, it appears, showed little emotion. He ordered his men to make camp, then rode with his officers to the ridge to see for himself. The last French contingent was coming to join force and the valley was crammed full. The road to Calais was completely cut off. By now it was late afternoon. Although the French were beginning to deploy their armies, Henry knew it was unlikely that battle would be joined before morning. Night would soon be here, and the enemy would not be foolish enough to allow him to remain in his superior position on the hillcrest. They would rather wait, employing their Fabian tactics in hopes of demoralizing his men; it would be necessary to go down across the ridge to meet them the next day. Swiftly Henry committed himself and his army to God, then ordered, in the last light, that all should ascend the ridge and see what he and the scout had seen. The chaplains began to pray and men, frightened, gathered round, begging for absolution, while Henry moved among them on the ridge. He spoke to them quietly, trying to cheer them. He remained serene, though it is probable that he was experiencing some of the trepidation which caused Sir Walter Hungerford to say that he wished they had ten thousand more archers with them. To this Henry replied:

Thou speakest foolishly, for by the God of Heaven, on whose grace I have relied, and in whom I have a firm hope of victory, I would not, even if I could, increase my number by one. For those whom I have are the people of God.

He assured Hungerford that these 'humble few' would be 'well able to conquer the haughty opposition of the French.'

They, for their part, were in high fettle. Here was the chance to avenge the crippling defeats of Crécy and Poitiers. More and more noble knights had joined the ranks which in the tree-lined valley were beginning to be blotted out by night and the teeming rain. Among the commanders, all beautifully mounted, heavily armed and jealous of their honour, were men such as Jacques de Châtillon, Seigneur de Dampierre and Admiral of France; the Sire de Rambures, who commanded the gunners; Guichard Dauphin, the Duke of Alençon, the Counts of Marle, Vendôme, Granpré and de Roucy, the Count of Fauquemberghes, Louis de Bourdon, Ganiot de Bournonville and Brunelet de Masinguëhen, the Sire de Lammartin, Clignet de Brébant and many, many more. Jean sans Peur, Duke of Burgundy, was ostensibly still at the christening feast which kept him diplomatically neutral, and his younger brother Antoine, Duke of Brabant had not yet arrived.

In the last rainfilled gleam, Henry commanded his army to leave the ridge and move down into the valley where the men billeted themselves in and round the village of Maisoncelles. Many of the peasants, like those from Agincourt and Tramecourt, had run away in fear. The French soldiers, over-excited at the prospect of a victorious battle, had made certain depredations, burning cottages and taking food and women, and there was little left in the way of provisions when Henry's party descended the hill. The lords' pavilions were set up, grooms and servants scurried about finding lodgings for their masters. Some of the men lay down on straw but the majority, especially the archers, the young English and Welsh boys, the Gascon mercenaries and the apprentice artisans, had to be content with the soaking muddy ground. They were now in the last stages of privation. For days they had eaten nothing but nuts and berries, and some were stricken with dysentery while those who had recovered succumbed again to the disease. There was a new sickness too sweeping through the camp – a heavy cold to add discomfort, and sneezing mingled with muted cursing. Almost everyone anticipated certain death in the morning. Their hunger was forgotten as soldier after soldier, alarmed for his soul, took turns in the line gathering beside every chaplain. Mingling with the murmur of confession and absolution from the overworked priests, the rain poured, relentless as fear.

As night came on, Henry sent round orders that absolute silence should be maintained within the camp. Earlier men had been racketing round shouting to one another in their search for billets, the armourers banging with hammer and file, and even the dogs and horses infected with noisy anxiety. He knew that the French were aware of the army's weakened state and it suited him that they should think it was in even worse case than was true, believing the men struck dumb with fear and privation or even that they had run away. He therefore threatened every knight with loss of horse and armour, and every inferior person with the loss of his right ear, and an obedient hush fell. This psychological ploy was

The lords' pavilions were set up.

partially successful; the French, who lay about three-quarters of a mile away, saw the campfires dying and the lack of movement and became mystified. Some commanders sent scouts through the woodland to try to ascertain the position.

For their part the enemy were noisy in the extreme. Their campfires flamed on the tree-boles and on the field of young corn which separated the two armies. Late into the night the sounds of carousal, merry shouts and laughter drifted on the wet wind as the French drank, ate and threw dice, wagering on the prisoners they would take tomorrow. The wagers varied with the value of the prize; the King and his brother of Gloucester were worth a six; a throw of five took other nobles such as York, Camoys, Oxford, and Huntingdon; skilled men were worth four; doctors and priests scored three and two; captains and sergeants one. The archers, of common peasant strain, were in French eyes worth nothing – a blank, for the French nobles despised even their own bowmen and were careful to segregate themselves from these, the proletariat. And so they jested, boasted and diced, and there was talk of painting a cart in which King Henry would be paraded captive through Paris when the battle was done.

And yet the feeling of faction still held sway, despite all this jollity. There were quarrels among lords and among their servants, boasts as to who owned the better right to lead the affray – whose blood was nobler, whose chivalry more profound, whose possessions greatest. In this fashion, and in the soaking quiet on the other edge of the field, midnight ushered in Friday, 25 October 1415, the feast of Sts Crispin and Crispinian.

These two saints, brothers, were famous throughout Europe during the Middle Ages. Towards the middle of the third century they came from Rome to preach in Gaul, and converted many. They set up residence at Soissons, where, imitating St Paul in manual labour, they worked by night making shoes, without payment from their customers, only insisting that their preaching was listened to. But complaints were lodged against them, and eventually, after various torments, the Emperor Maximian ordered them to be beheaded.

A church dedicated to St Crépin-le-Petit was built over their tomb and St Eligius the Smith embellished their shrine. They are the traditional patrons of shoemakers and leather-workers of all kinds, and are represented in art with the symbols of their shoemakers' trade, but all information about them is vague. One theory is that they were Roman martyrs, whose relics were brought to Soissons and thus begot a *cultus* there. The church at Soissons certainly exhibited a considerable number of their bones during the Middle Ages, but very few have survived.

A tradition exists that they fled to escape persecutions to Faversham in Kent, where they pursued their trade and preaching at the site of the Swan Inn, Preston Street, 'near the Cross Well'. An altar was dedicated to them in the parish church of St Mary of Charity.

On the night of their feast the rain fell steadily, making the field, already trodden by the host of French feet, hooves and and wheels, into a quagmire. While the singing and shouting filtered across, more and more English made what they believed to be their last confession and were given the Eucharist. A feeling of absolute doom settled on them, and this the King, dressed like an ordinary soldier, set out to alleviate in the manner Shakespeare describes:

> O, now, who will behold
> The royal captain of this ruin'd band,
> Walking from watch to watch, from tent to tent,
> Let him cry – Praise and glory on his head!
> For forth he goes, and visits all his host;
> Bids them good morrow, with a modest smile:
> And calls them – brothers, friends, and countrymen.
> Upon his royal face there is no note
> How dread an army hath enrounded him . . .
>
> . . . His liberal eye doth give to every one,
> Thawing cold fear, that mean and gentle all
> Behold (as may unworthiness define)
> A little touch of Harry in the night . . .

He spoke to his archers, dispiritedly waxing their strings and notching arrows; to his craftsmen, clerks, yeomen and doctors, to Master George Benet and his fellow cordwainers whose patrons' day this was. Flanked by his night-guards Guy Midelton and John Melton he went through the lines, directing the shivering small groups to remember that they were all in the hands of God. It would have been unthinkable for him to do otherwise and it is impossible to believe that the men were not to some extent comforted, as were Gloucester, Erpingham, Camoys, Umfraville, Hungerford, Salisbury, Cornwall, Greyndon, Sir Richard Kyghley, York, Dafydd ap Llywelyn ap Hywel, and Michael de la Pole, the young Earl of Suffolk whose father had died of dysentery at Harfleur. His calmness pervaded the deathly fear-filled night. He was still adamant that his cause had Divine approval despite the desperate odds, and his conviction communicated itself to others. This was King Henry at his best, cool, assured, an inspiration that bred tranquillity so that old soldiers comforted young, and men were able to snatch an hour of sleep.

His tranquillity was fatalistic. Earlier, upon registering the tremendous adversary from the ridge, he had sent emissaries across the field asking once more for a safe passage to Calais, and he had in fact agreed with reluctance to surrender Harfleur as part of the bargain. It was a hopeless attempt: the French replied that he should surrender not only Harfleur but also his claim to the French crown and all remaining English possessions. Once again they stated that he had no rights. And it was all too late; they were out for his blood. The battle was to be joined at dawn, which came with a final gust of rain that cleared to light the morass ahead.

Henry went then and put on his full armour, but left his head bare so that the men should see his face clearly when the time came to address them. Over his armour he wore his côte d'armes, the three gold leopards of England on a red ground quartered with the three gold lilies of France on a blue ground.

The story of the gift of the fleurs-de-lis to France, according to a legend referred to by Raoul de Presles and dating from the 14th century, describes God sending an angel bearing a cloth embroidered with three fleurs-de-lis to a hermit. Clotilde, wife of Clovis, King of the Franks, gave alms to the hermit and in return he handed her the cloth, telling her to give it to her husband, who put it on the shield he bore against the Saracens. This legend is illustrated in the *Bedford Book of Hours*, written in Paris about 1415.

During the night Henry had sent scouts to survey the field and they had reported it as fairly favourable to the English. The great French force was still hemmed in upon itself by the woods of Tramecourt and Agincourt in an antique battle-plan which relied on sheer weight and force and denied the participants any free disposition of movement within the area. In any case the commanders, themselves too numerous, could not hope to control the movements of such a vast, disparate and quarrelsome army. The lessons of Crécy and Poitiers were, after all, forgotten. The surrounding trees were a far greater hindrance and hazard than they realized. In their dawn position they had a frontal area of no more than three-quarters of a mile in which to fight, and any advance on their part would narrow this front to about half a mile where the flanking woods grew inward. The enormous proud force was already jostling banner upon banner in the early light. Arguments over who was to take precedence in line sharpened. Some of the chevaliers had spent the night in the saddle rather than foul their gleaming armour in the mud, and those who had been drinking and roistering were short-tempered.

Henry heard Mass in his pavilion and then emerged to draw up his troops. His advantage became immediately evident to him and the commanders. With its back to the Maisoncelles wood, his force was relatively so small and the field so much wider than that occupied by the enemy that he was able to position the archers and foot-soldiers in the most diverse yet economical way possible. He formed the men into one line (there were none left for reserves), and they stood four deep in the conventional three divisions with the King commanding the centre, the Duke of York on the right, and Lord Camoys on the left. Alternating with each of these divisions were the archers in a formation known as a herse or harrow, a series of split triangles which converged where each formation was placed side to side. These triangular wedges continued outwards on either flank, where bowmen stood four or five deep and the tip of each wedge pointed at the adversary. Thus the archers were able to fire in any direction and, so deployed under the command of Sir Thomas Erpingham, each man stood with his longbow and arrows and the sharp stake laboriously carried for the past eight days.

The saddled horses were led to the back of the lines and the wagons full of baggage and wounded men were taken for safety to the woods. The trumpeters in the minstrel band raised their bannered instruments – John Cliff, Thomas Norys Tromper, Panel and Peut Trumper, Meysham, Broune and Richard Pyper – musicians who played for the King in times of peace ready now to sound the call of war. The deployment of the army was carried out still in absolute silence. Sir John Cornwall's thirteen-year-old son looked on tensely from the baggage park. Pennons and standards were raised and Henry, now seated on a grey palfrey, commanded the royal banner with the arms of Our Lady, the Trinity and St George to be unfurled above his head. Sir John Codrington was Henry's standard-bearer. He bore as arms three red lions on a silver field and a red fess (the centre third of a shield). Later as a reward for his services in the battle, he was permitted to show the fess 'embattled' – looking like the crenellated top of a castle wall. 'Now is good time,' the King announced, 'for all England prays for us. Let us be of good cheer therefore and go to our journey.' It was just on Prime (6.0 a.m.), the first canonical hour of Crispin's Day.

Across the field the French host waited, already in some disarray in their immense deep line. The commanders previously appointed by d'Albret and Boucicaut were being

The inner side of Henry V's shield, and his saddle.

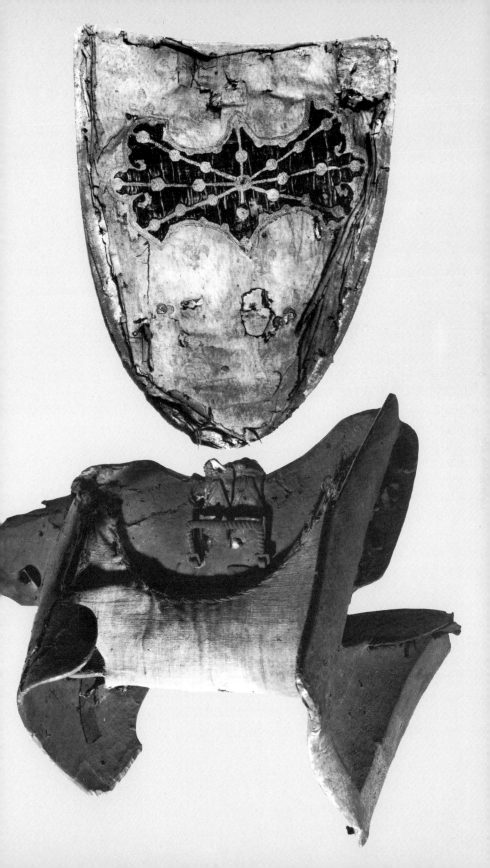

forced aside as scores of noble knights pushed jealously to the forefront, thoughts of personal prestige overriding those of tactics; the crossbowmen who had been deployed on the wings were nudged further into the cramping woodland and the artillery suffered the same fate, being effectively masked by the trees. The front line of unmounted knights surged and bulged untidily. Every moment another potential leader burst into the line which eventually came to consist of Bourbon, d'Albret, who managed to maintain his command next to Marshal Boucicaut, while close by the Duke of Orléans's banner with the Armagnac porcupine and fleurs-de-lis bristled on the air. The Counts of Eu and Richemont and countless other commanders such as Sire Ferry de Lorraine bolstered and nudged one another, so that Louis de Bourdon and the Count of Vendôme were pushed further outward to the wings. The Dukes of Alençon and Bar occupied the second line. The rearguard consisted of cavalry commanded by Lammartin, Marle and Fauquemberghes, a powerful contingent like that which had flattened Henry's archers at Corbie and deputed now to ride them down again. The great warhorses were unarmoured save for the occasional steel headpiece, and wore gay silk housings in colours as brilliant and diffuse as the many banners jostling overhead. There was no sign of the Duke of Brittany despite previous promises, nor of Burgundy who had remained at his christening feast uncommitted. Somewhere in the centre of the crammed front line Guillaume Martel raised, with difficulty, the oriflamme standard.

It seemed that a solid wall of silver-grey, broken by colours of shameless loveliness, confronted the English. It was a legion of steel. The hundreds of counts and dukes were living carapaces, encased from head to foot in bolted metal. Their great helmets had chain aventails riveted at the base, imprisoning the wearer's neck. Steel plate cast about legs met steel boots at the ankle. Hands in gloves of boiled leather were weighted further by mailed gauntlets. Shining elbow-joints met thick rings of chain mail and merged into steel rivets at the shoulder. Nearly all the knights bore upwards of fifty pounds of armour, not counting the heavy weapons carried. The helm and cuirass alone of the Sire Ferry de Lorraine weighed ninety pounds. The nobles seemed to outnumber the common soldiery by reason of their giant splendour. The line was a steelbound serpent, undulating and reforming as jealous pride pushed man and beast against one another; metal grated on metal and the bright standards intertwined. And time and again, as the daylight grew and sun replaced the rain, quarrels broke out between the partisans of Burgundy and Armagnac.

For some three hours the two armies stood facing one another, neither making any attempt to advance, the French astonished that the mere sight of such force did not cause an immediate surrender, and Henry loath to move forward and relinquish any of the wide territory he occupied away from the trees. Glancing round at his little army, he realized that time was running out. The men were primed for the effort of battle but they were also in the last stages of endurance and further delay could only undermine them. He saw how ragged they were, how dirty, dogged, hungry and brave. Some of the archers had no breeches at all, and their bare legs were chapped with rain. They were shoeless, gloveless, pale and desperate. He had marched them to death and near-death and still they stood silently waiting to do his will. He left the little grey palfrey and the groom, Gerard de la Strade, brought forward a magnificent snow-white horse for him to mount. He called the priests to the forefront. After hearing another Mass, he took from his armourer his bascinet which was plated with gold and encircled by the crown. Made of pure gold, the fleurons were studded with rubies, sapphires and 128 pearls. In the centre of the diadem shone the Black Prince's great spinel ruby. He instructed Dean Edmund Lacy and his priests to pray loudly.

Remember us, O Lord! Our enemies are gathered together and boast in their might. Scatter their strength and disperse them,

that they may know that there is none other that fighteth for us
but only thou, our God.

Henry then addressed the men, saying:

that he was come into France to recover his lawful inheritance
and that he had good and just cause to claim it, and in that quarrel
they might freely and surely fight; that they should remember
they were born in the Kingdom of England where their fathers
and mothers, wives and children now dwelt and therefore they
ought to strive to return there with great glory and fame; that
the Kings of England, his predecessors, had gained many noble
victories over the French; and that on that day every man present
should do his utmost to preserve his own honour and the honour
of the Crown of England.

He then directed his address primarily towards the archers,
telling them what his spies had discovered during the night:
that the French planned to cripple every archer taken alive
by severing three fingers of his right hand so that never again
could he draw a bow. Afterwards the archers would be sold
in bunches of twenty as slaves. The word was passed back,
and a ripple of indignation shook the quiet ranks. Longbows
were gripped tighter; the King's final words put the men
further on their mettle: he shouted that he would never be
taken prisoner but would rather die than charge England
with the payment of his ransom. At the end the army cheered
him, saying: 'Sir, we pray that God give you a good life, and
victory over your foes.'

Once more they waited, while the French stood still across
the field, mightily armoured men with their heavy swords
and lances, some broken off short for easier wielding in the
crush. The great horses were so burdened by the weight of
their mailed riders that their feet sank fetlock-deep in the
mud. Still the French showed no impatience to begin but
remained confident, jocular, some still quarrelling, others
calling to their fellows for forgiveness for past insults, some
eating and drinking. Henry, knowing that the high tenor of
his restless men must be maintained, called for Sir Thomas

English archers fighting in close formation.

Erpingham to ready the archers. The knight moved back along the line. It was by now about eleven in the morning.

Erpingham ascertained that the wedge-shaped formations were tightly aligned. He saw how unprotected the archers were. Some were not only ragged, they were, like the Irish contingent, naked except for their belt stuck with clubs and arrows. Many had lost their hats of wickerwork and iron, their sole protection against the enemy weapons. When they

were ready, Erpingham threw his baton in the air, crying
'*Nestroque!*' the word of marshal's command meaning either:
'Now, strike!' or 'Knee! Stretch!' and was answered by a
shout from the bowmen. He then placed himself beside the
King who, with banners raised above him, stood, now dismounted, at the head of his men-at-arms. Henry ordered his
chaplains to pray again and directed the heralds to their position. He then formally cried battle:

'Banner, avaunt! In the Name of Jesus, Mary, and St
George!'

All round him the men-at-arms bore the device of St
George, the red cross blazoned on their surcoats, as if this
were part of the Holy War for which Henry's heart still
longed. Men dipped and knelt, hearing the battle-cry, signing
the ground with the Cross, then taking a handful of mud to
their lips. 'As I, O God, came of dust, let this be Thy Sacrament, and should I fall, let me return to Him who made
me . . .'

Some chroniclers attest that a vision of St George was seen
in the sky over the field; a phenomenon akin to the Three
Suns seen by Edward IV at Mortimers Cross, and to the
Angels of Mons in World War I, explicable either as a romantic embellishment or a genuine mass hallucination caused by
heightened excitement. Such stories abound in the theatre of
war.

The men rose, and in its three tight divisions the army
marched forward. The small host seemed to diminish the
nearer it came to the monstrous wall of steel ahead. As the
gap narrowed to a range of 300 yards and the French were
within bowshot, the trumpets sounded and every archer ran
forward and planted the sharp stake at an angle towards the
enemy, running back to notch his arrow along the greased
string. There was plenty of space, even in the neat 'harrows',
to draw the fletch back to the ear and feel the sixty pounds'
weight of the hauled string. The *chevaux de frise* stood firm
from the flanks to the centre, where the King, York and
Camoys, now dismounted, came on with drawn swords.

158

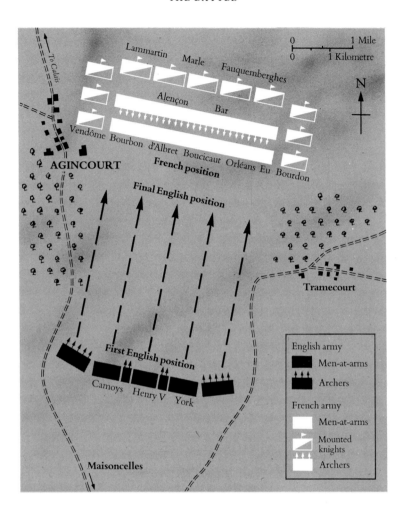

The French and English dispositions at Agincourt.

French horsemen began galloping round from the wings.
At sight of the English advance, Charles d'Albret uttered the
battle-cry: '*Montjoie! Montjoie! St Denis!*' Guillaume Martel
moved forward with the scarlet banner beating the air. The
steel wall undulated and began its advance. French faces could
be seen under arrogantly raised visors. Behind the leaders (in
the front line there were at least twenty seeking precedence

and d'Albret and Boucicaut were struggling for command), the deep rows of foot-soldiers clustered haphazardly, groping for a place. Hampered by the thrusting of the knights, the crossbowmen in between and on the flanks were awkwardly trying to maintain some kind of order, loading the clumsy, intricate weapons while being pushed towards the trees. On either side the artillery was likewise hindered, and men under the command of Rambures found it difficult to load their cannon as the tight-packed cavalry came sweeping round. This, the task force set solely to destroy the English archers, came on at a lumbering gallop across the field, the riders' brilliant armour dulled at last by flecks of upthrown mud, while under the oriflamme an innumerable force of knights like gigantic robots strode forward, the front line comprising the flower of French chivalry. Others pushed wildly at them from behind. The charging cavalry gathered speed.

The young archers stood with their eyes on the lifted baton of Thomas Erpingham. A race memory roared within them, of practice at the butts performed every Sunday by their fathers and grandfathers, culminating in their own acquisition of skill which now held them fast, tense, notched. The horses came nearer; great pounding hooves splashed among the clay. The roar of *Montjoie!* rose in crescendo. Sir Thomas tossed his baton high. Trumpets screamed. The sky became black with surging English arrows.

It was as if premature night had blown up on a hurricane or a million birds flying at top speed had suddenly filled the air and shadowed the field, the noise of their wings almost drowning the battle-cries: 'For Harry! For Jesus! *Montjoie! St Denis!*' Flight after flight of arrows was launched as the horsemen thundered down to crush once and for all the despised creatures unfit to do battle with the lords of France. The charge had nearly reached its goal when the leaders saw the *chevaux de frise*, which had blended innocuously with the surrounding clay. They tore desperately on the bridles in a vain effort to control the spurred, excited horses. Impetus carried the charge on to the stakes. Horses were spitted

Knights and yeomen battled side by side: Gloucester, Huntingdon, Cornwall, Suffolk, the one-eyed Davy Gam, the young Welsh boys, the foreign mercenaries, the gunners and artisans, all threw themselves into the mêlée. The bowmen went to work with axes and broken lances. Soon, deep piles of corpses towered higher than a man's head. The archers leaped on to these pyramids, swooping down to slash at the throats of felled Frenchmen. The mud was red; mailed feet slithered in lakes of blood, while the archers' bare legs were scarlet and the little naked Irishmen, howling war-cries, looked as if they had rolled in a slaughterhouse. The mighty advance had been ruined by its own splendour, and across the field a flock of horrified French could be seen in retreat. Other contingents in the rearguard milled aimlessly about; they had been given no orders. The cannon remained silent, and the crossbowmen had long since given up trying to load their antique weapons. Many were deserting.

In face of these disastrous events, what remained of the advance continued to fight bravely. Packed together, groaning and slipping in the mud, knowing that to fall down was death, they struck out desperately, trying to parry the sword-thrusts of the English men-at-arms and the manic hammerings of the excited archers who skipped about on bare feet wielding halberds and maces. Stunned noblemen found themselves hauled away to be held for ransom. It was becoming difficult to move about the field as fresh heaps of dead and wounded gathered. The archers were looting, tearing off gauntlets to snatch jewels from fingers, slicing off the fingers themselves in grim reprisal for the earlier French threat, and tearing off cuirasses to get at the jewelled collars beneath. Among the prisoners taken were Marshal Boucicaut, the fabulously wealthy Armagnac partisan the Duke of Bourbon, and the Counts of Richemont, Eu and Vendôme. Taken by Henry's escort was the young Duke Charles of Orléans, the principal figurehead of the Armagnac party.

Henry himself, it is agreed, performed prodigious feats of heroism, fighting so valiantly that some remarked that even

The Battle of Agincourt, from a fifteenth-century French manuscript.

had he been of inferior rank he would have earned himself greater renown than any other soldier. There is an uncorroborated story that he dressed two other men in similar armour with crowned helmets to confuse the enemy; yet the fact that he exposed himself to common danger is uncontestable, and he was at one point nearly killed. During a lull in the fighting when the archers, drunk with triumph and temporarily concerned only with plunder, were off guard, a flock of eighteen knights who had sworn to capture Henry's crown or die swept down on the King. Led by Brunelet de Masinguëhen and Ganiot de Bournonville, they blundered with raised weapons through the mailed mounds. The Household knights engaged them in combat but were unable to prevent a sword from landing obliquely on the King's head so that one of the gold fleurons of the crown was broken off and his bascinet dented. Evidence of this blow can be seen on the helmet above his tomb in Westminster Abbey.

Meanwhile, a second line of French came forward in an

untidy, desperate wave. The fighting went on unabated with much the same results as previously. This charge was led by the Duke of Alençon, who had galloped off to apprehend the deserters and who, with this fresh force, smashed down on one of the pockets of combat where Humphrey, Duke of Gloucester was embattled with the men of Marle and Fauquemberghes who had both so far remained unharmed. A wild knife-thrust from one of Alençon's escort pierced Gloucester's belly beneath his cuirass and he fell wounded. Hearing of this, Henry was quickly at his side with a bodyguard of archers and yeomen, men like Dafydd ap Llywelyn ap Hywel who shot and clubbed out a path for him, and his son-in-law Richard Vaughan of Bredwardine. It is said that Henry stood astride his brother's body, protecting him until the danger was past. It was perhaps at this moment that the Welshman and his son-in-law who had fought like fiends fell mortally wounded.

The Duke of Alençon, his men dead and dying round him, limped forward towards Henry, stretching out his sword in token of surrender, and calling 'I yield!' Before Henry could give him his hand in assent, one of the Household, blind with zeal and seeing only the drawn sword, leaped between them. His axe spun across the Duke's throat and Alençon's head whirled into the mud at their feet. At the same time, Dafydd ap Llywelyn ap Hywel lay bleeding, supported by his pages, and Henry went to him. Applauding his valour, he touched him on either shoulder with a sword. 'In the Name of the Father, Son, and Holy Ghost, I create thee a knight,' he said, and Davy Gam, who as brother-in-law of Owain Glyn Dŵr had once fought in Wales against the young Henry, died in his service. Richard Vaughan was also knighted.

Within half an hour the little army had thrust its way through the French ranks, scrambling over mountained bodies in the bloody mud. More and more French, aghast at their comrades' fate, were running away, mounting loose horses or lumbering into the trees, casting off pieces of armour the better to flee. Archers and yeomen continued to plunder the piles of dead and wounded, seeking out, through their côtes d'armes, men of noble family still left alive and dragging some of these off to huts on the edge of the woodland for later ransom. To the French this was the most ignominious part. The cream of their chivalry was falling into the hands of peasants, men who in their eyes were lower than worms. Pockets of fighting continued, most of the strife being concentrated near to Henry. The young Michael de la Pole, Earl of Suffolk, and Sir Richard Kyghley became two of the rare English casualties, both being killed in hand-to-hand combat. The stout Edward of York battled against Charles d'Albret, who with commendable courage had stood his ground to fight desperately on. Lord Camoys, Huntingdon, Sir John Cornwall, Erpingham, Umfraville and others continued to stab and strike and thrust. Soon after noon the field was almost completely covered with slain French; the pattern of battle had disappeared, and there were no lines, wedges or formations. The English moved in almost leisurely fashion between the heaps of dead. Prisoners worth thousands of pounds in ransom were being led away. The third line of mounted men-at-arms in the distance began, horrified, to disperse towards Ruisseauville. Carrion crows circled overhead as the English continued looting. Even the men guarding the baggage wagons left their posts to join in search of spoil. This negligence provoked the loss of some of the King's valuables, for a rabble of French peasants, led by three knights, plundered the wagons, taking several horses, a jewelled crown, the Chancery Seals, and some gold and silver. There is no evidence whatever of the baggage-boys being slaughtered as Shakespeare would have us believe. These boys were little more than children and such an act would have been not only wildly unchivalrous, but pointless.

Suddenly the lull was shattered by a surprise assault from Antoine, Duke of Brabant, younger brother of the absent Duke of Burgundy. Directly contravening his brother's orders not to become involved in the battle, he joined it late, bringing a few Burgundian knights and all the followers he could muster from the group of men among the trees. As he hastened to face the unbelievable carnage that lay before him he saw some of the escort of the captured Charles of Orléans, and called to them to support him. Brabant had come in such a hurry he had forgotten to put on his côte d'armes and the knights stared at him without recognition. He identified himself and received the cold answer that Armagnac did not fight for Burgundy. Even at that desperate juncture, old rivalries superseded the common good.

Brabant looked wildly round for something to wear over his armour and seized the banner from a trumpet borne by his herald. Cutting a hole in the cloth, he struggled into this makeshift tabard and rode forward. He charged straight into a mêlée dominated by King Henry and was unhorsed within minutes, his person given over to a grinning foot-soldier and most of his men dead or dying round him.

Although it now seemed to the army that all danger was past, Henry had been keeping a close watch on the broken lines of French waiting in the trees. He saw the colours of the Duke of Marle and the Count of Fauquemberghes, both of whom were readying themselves for a last desperate charge. He saw also how his own archers and foot-soldiers were unwarily taking their ease, some sitting on the prone steel forms of their victims, all gloating and drunk with incredulous rapture. On the edge of the field and half-hidden by woodland were thousands of men-at-arms and bowmen of the first two French battalions who could return at any moment. Moreover, the number of French prisoners greatly exceeded that of their captors, and not all had been disarmed. Marle and Fauquemberghes in the distance had managed to muster about six hundred men; not without difficulty, for just as Armagnacs refused to obey the commands of Burgundians, Gascons, Bretons and Poitevins whose commanders had been killed were refusing to serve under a strange banner. Yet the

OVERLEAF: *French and English in battle.*

force was there, a tangible threat, and the English army was for the moment unquestionably off its guard. Henry saw clearly that at any time they might need to fight again, and that the prisoners could well turn on their captors while they were thus engaged. It was a situation of great potential danger, and he was determined above all things that the victory so nearly his should not be jeopardized. He therefore ordered that most of the prisoners should be killed.

Latter-day historians have condemned Henry for this butchery. The nineteenth-century French scholar René de Belleval declared that 'this barbaric act left an indelible stain on the honour of England.' It must, however, be remembered that this again, as with the banishment of the infirm of Harfleur, was a case of medieval expediency. Scattered and diffused though the enemy were, they could, given leaders, easily have formed a party of retaliation and those leaders, Marle and Fauquemberghes, were by now riding across the field towards Henry. The two noblemen had been inspired by the brave and hopeless charge of the Duke of Brabant. In fact, many Frenchmen were later to curse Brabant for that lunatic foray which, they maintained, indirectly caused the execution of the prisoners.

Implicit in Henry's order was that the members of the ducal houses should be spared. Yet all other lives were forfeit and the English yeomen, staring down at the wealthy landowners they had captured, grumbled at the loss of ransoms. The Duke of Brabant's captor raised his sword. Rich, royal, yet still unrecognizable in his makeshift garment, the Duke died like a common man, his throat slashed through by one.

Some of the men in the English army came nearer to mutiny at this point than at any time before. The thought of forfeiting the precious ransoms went hard with them, and some began openly to refuse to obey orders. Henry, seeing the preparations for a charge being made by Marle and Fauquemberghes, threatened to hang any man who disobeyed, and deputed 200 archers to perform wholesale executions of the hostages. His threat took effect. In a few moments thousands of French were stabbed to the heart or had their throats cut. Beside those who had suffocated in their own armour or beneath the crushing bodies of their companions, this slaughter rather than active combat appears to have accounted for the great number of final dead.

Even some of the prisoners lying bound or wounded in the huts on the edge of the trees or in villagers' houses did not escape but had their dwelling set on fire over their heads. One such knight, Sire Gilbert de Lannoy, who was afterwards to become Philip of Burgundy's Chamberlain and emissary to the Holy Land, was luckier than most. He managed to attract the attention of Sir John Cornwall, and by convincing him of his personal nobility and value was spared and hidden until the battle was over. The ransom later collected by Sir John amounted to 1200 crowns and a fine war-horse.

Perhaps this mass murder was unnecessary after all; it is impossible to say. However, as it happened the charge of Marle and Fauquemberghes turned out to be a half-hearted affair resulting in defeat, both noblemen being soon killed and their supporters who escaped death quickly fleeing the field. This last skirmish none the less claimed the life of one of Henry's prominent knights: the ex-traitor, the fat and scheming Edward, Duke of York. When the towers of slain were finally dismantled, York's corpulent body was found at the bottom of a heap, unwounded but smothered by the vast, splendidly armoured corpses of several Frenchmen. Like Charles d'Albret, also found dead, York had been in the front line of the confrontation.

Thus the final gap was mended and the battle, which had lasted about three hours, was over. As King and army, almost too stupefied as yet to realize their full triumph, gazed over the bloody, corpse-strewn field, the carrion birds drifted down to feast on the dead. Smoke from the burning huts blackened the perimeter. Occasionally a prone shape moaned, heaved and stilled. It was the early afternoon of Crispin's Day. Now that day belonged for ever to King Henry V. God had given him the victory.

O God, thy arm was here,
And not to us, but to thy arm alone,
Ascribe we all. – When, without stratagem,
But in plain shock and even play of battle,
Was ever known so great and little loss,
On one part and on the other? – Take it, O God,
For it is none but thine!

SHAKESPEARE: *King Henry V*,
Act IV, Sc. 8

Aftermath

Henry walked over the dead-strewn field, where for the remainder of the day the army worked ceaselessly, stripping clothes and armour from the corpses, searching for articles of value such as gem-hilted daggers, gold ornaments, rings, brooches and coins, rounding up the frightened loose horses and appropriating them (their value to be divided later through syndicates ruling plunder), trying on pieces of fine Italian steel harness, some of it dented by blows and twisted out of shape by the frenzy of the past three hours.

The very few French found alive were quickly despatched with blades, although some had managed to crawl from the field into the ditches and woodlands where most of them died during the night. Looting became an obsession; every soldier loaded himself with more clothes, trinkets and armour than he could reasonably hope to carry on the march to Calais, to which the road now lay open at last.

In no way did Henry see his triumph as a personal victory. It was and always had been God's cause. The incredibly ill-chosen tactics and manœuvres of the French, the disputes between the leaders and the lack of discipline which had brought them to disaster, were in his eyes incidental to the purpose

Banquets such as this were prepared for the conqueror's homecoming.

God had mapped out for him. The vision of St George remained; the hand of God and his saints had upheld the army. His trust had never been confounded, and it is unlikely that he had ever imagined it would be, save perhaps in that one bad moment before the battle when he had offered to surrender Harfleur. Now he called before him Montjoie, Principal Herald of France. In his pavilion, in the presence of his own heralds, Leicester, Guienne and Chester, Ireland King of Arms, Antelope Pursuivant, and Hereford Marshal of Arms, he formally demanded to whom the victory belonged, and Montjoie conceded France's defeat. Henry reiterated sternly that all this slaughter had been forced upon him by the French, and that the catastrophe had been self-administered through their withholding his just and rightful inheritance. He asked Montjoie the name of the castle beyond the woods northwest of the battlefield. On being informed, he declared that as all battles should' by tradition be named after the fortress nearest to which they were fought, this should for all time be known as the battle of Agincourt. At the present day the castle no longer stands, and the name has been changed to Azincourt, but the bloody terrain of the Somme valley and its environs where so many men have since fought and died remains relatively unaltered.

Towards the day's end the rain started again, and the King and army moved back to their billets at Maisoncelles, where, after hearing a Mass, he sat down to supper. As at Harfleur, his implacable pride was evident, for he ordered that the noblest of the French prisoners, among them Charles of Orléans and the Duke of Bourbon, should act as servitors at his table. In his usual vein and pompous if incontrovertible style he lectured them, emphasizing that God had given the victory to His chosen people.

Outside, the now silent field was lit by a fierce fire. The English dead had been placed in a large barn on the edge of Maisoncelles, together with loot which had by now reached ridiculous proportions and had caused the King to order that no soldier should retain more armour than he could wear himself, for the loads of plunder would have made the journey to Calais impossible and would have sunk the ships that were to bear the army home. The barn, together with all contents and wagonloads of fresh booty still coming from the field, was set ablaze. The stench of leather and cloth and burning flesh was nauseating. Only the slain lords – Edward of York, the Earl of Suffolk and others – were kept from the pyre, their flesh being boiled from their bones which were then packed in chests ready for shipment home and burial.

The French dead, now being scavenged by their own countrymen, peasants who had crept back to the villages, were left to lie. The firelight flickered weirdly on the naked blood-streaked white bodies. Some of the wealthier families had sent servants to bring home the dead, and countless others

Some of the wealthier families sent servants to bring home the dead.

were taken to the cemeteries at Agincourt, Hesdin, or Ruisseauville until these were unable to house any more. Wolves
came in to forage among the remainder, and birds pecked out
eyes as the flamelit dusk came down. Eventually a great pit,
nearly twenty-five yards square, was dug for the bodies, and
here 6000 were placed, the common grave being blessed and
planted round with a thick thorn hedge as a protection against
wolves. Today a memorial erected by the lords of Tramecourt marks the spot. In the eighteenth century the Marquise
de Tramecourt built a chapel there as a token of thanksgiving
for her son's safe return from war. Sixty years later agents of
the French Revolution destroyed it, but during World War
II the Comte de Tramecourt and his son led the local Resistance from this site, both dying later in a German concen-
tration camp.

In the general confusion and varying disposal of the corpses
on both sides, it is extremely difficult to assess the exact num-
bers killed. However, whatever the conclusion, nothing de-
tracts from the miraculous victory of the English against
unprecedented odds. Contemporary sources place the French
dead between 4000 and 11,000, while two modern historians,
one French, one English, say 7000 and 10,000 respectively,
and the truth probably lies in between. French prisoners taken
numbered approximately 1600; besides Orléans, Bourbon
and Boucicaut, the Counts of Richemont, Eu and Vendôme
were captured.

Of the English casualties, not all of them mortal, the most
reliable estimate is the incredibly low figure of one hundred.
Out of this number there appears to be only a handful of
noblemen and knights: other than Suffolk, York, Kyghley,
Thomas Fitzhenry, John de Peniton, Walter Lord and Sir
Dafydd ap Llywelyn ap Hywel, most were archers or foot-
soldiers.

But the flower of France had sustained a savage blow. René
de Belleval writes: '*Jamais désastre aussi grand n'avait été infligé
à la France. Courtray, Crécy et Poitiers etaient surpassés.*' ('Never
had France suffered so great a disaster. It surpassed Courtrai,
Crécy and Poitiers.')

Charles d'Albret, Constable of France, had fought his last battle. Dead also were Jacques de Châtillon, Seigneur de Dampierre, Admiral of France; the Artillery Master, the Sire de Rambures; Guichard Dauphin, Grand Hospitaller to King Charles; Antoine, Duke of Brabant and his brother the Count of Nevers, Dukes Edouard de Bar, Alençon and Marle, Ferry de Lorraine, Jean de Bar, the Sire de Puisaye, the Counts of Blamont, Granpré, de Roucy, Fauquemberghes, Louis de Bourdon and thousands of others, a chivalry too numerous to name. The bright banners, the gaudy côtes d'armes, had flashed and fluttered in vain.

Much to the satisfaction of Jean sans Peur, Duke of Burgundy, the Armagnac faction suffered greatly through the battle. Its two main leaders, Charles of Orléans and the Duke of Bourbon, were destined to be taken to England. Bourbon, together with Marshal Boucicaut, was immured in Pontefract Castle and died in England, while Charles of Orléans was kept a prisoner in the Tower of London for some twenty-five years, during which time he occupied himself writing reams of beautiful, melancholy verse. The Count of Eu also remained a prisoner for twenty years in England. Christine de Pisan, the Italian court poetess, dedicated an epic poem of consolation to Marie de Berry, wife of the Duke of Bourbon and mother of the Count of Eu, describing in lyric terms the full tragedy sustained by the noble families of France.

On the following morning, 26 October, after hearing a celebratory Mass and making offerings of thanksgiving, the King and his troops, no longer wearing their côtes d'armes, left Maisoncelles and passed with their captives over the torn red field. There, among the corpses, a few naked wounded Frenchmen struggled in vain to hide. Those too badly injured to move were swiftly killed, while others who could walk were clothed after a fashion and taken along on the Calais road. All the English horses and those plundered from the French were loaded down with booty, mostly weapons and other military equipment from the once-glorious force. It was only forty miles to Calais but the going was slow, about

*Charles of Orléans, captured at Agincourt, imprisoned
in the Tower of London.*

twelve miles a day. The overloaded army was exhausted and food was again a problem, exacerbated by the fact that prisoners as well as men had to be foraged for. It was still raining, and a sense of anti-climax began to attack the marchers. Perhaps something of the sort was also felt by Henry. It was true that he had achieved a momentous victory against staggering odds, but he was wise and far-sighted enough to realize that winning this one battle had not enhanced his gains in France. The King and Dauphin remained, after all, sovereign and heir respectively. Henry was returning home with tales of glory and a few ransoms from this costly expedition. His inheritance, the lands and castles and fiefs – his *raison d'être* for the whole campaign – were still far from his grasp. He knew intuitively that the smarting shame he had inflicted on the great French houses would not be borne lightly and that future reprisals would unquestionably have to be faced. Agincourt was merely the start of a long struggle. He would need to return to France as soon as he could find fresh funds to marshal and equip another army. To the noble prisoners, despairingly borne along in the train, he showed no sign of this mental burden, however, and when the army was encamped at nights, he spent some time talking to these captives. He treated them chivalrously, sending them food from his own table, but he appears to have lectured them constantly, rubbing salt in their wounded pride in a tiresome manner.

'Noble cousin, be of good heart,' he said to the Duke of Orléans.

I know that God gave me the victory over the French, not that I deserved it. But I fully believe that He wished to punish my enemies; and that, if what I have heard be true, it is not to be wondered at, for never were there greater disorders, sensuality and vices seen than now prevail in France, which it is horrible to hear described. And if God is provoked, no one can be surprised by it.

It is not surprising either to learn that the prisoners kept out of Henry's way as much as possible until they reached

Guisnes, where the King installed them and himself in the castle, directing the army to march to Calais alone. At Guisnes, Henry had the opportunity to question Orléans on the state of the faction between Burgundy and Armagnac, and perhaps heard rumours of the Dauphin Louis's increasing ill-health (he was to die in mysterious circumstances within a short time). Already Henry had decided that if his claims to France were to be achieved, Burgundy was the party to be wooed rather than that of the Orléanists, now depleted by the loss of several leaders.

Six miles away at Calais the jaded army, far from reaping any reward for their heroics, were hard put to find lodgings. The town was crammed with their compatriots, and shortage of provisions made wealthy men of the merchants who extorted the highest prices for all commodities. Shiploads of meat, fish, flour and beer had been promised from London but had not yet arrived. The soldiers, desperate for food and rest, found themselves forced to sell their hard-won hostages, their booty and their armour in order to survive. Many French prisoners changed hands for a tenth of their true value, and were re-sold immediately by the citizens of Calais to representatives of the English nobility or to ecclesiastical houses in England, and were destined to spend many years bound in such service far from home.

Ships from Dover and Sandwich had been summoned to fetch the army back, but by now the first of the winter storms was battering the Channel and the vessels were delayed for several days. When Henry finally entered Calais on 29 October the army was aching to leave France, and certain rumours circulating were causing some disquiet. It was already whispered that the King had plans for the men, tired out though they were, if not to march straightway to Paris, then to attack Ardres, a stronghold outside the Calais Pale. He did in fact put this proposition to his war councillors whom he had overruled at Harfleur, but was met with such stern opposition that he abandoned the project.

In splendour he entered Calais, accompanied by its Captain, the Earl of Warwick, all the clergy and the leading citizens who had ridden out to meet him. Richly vested, the canons and singing-boys chanted the *Te Deum Laudamus* and the English people cheered: 'Welcome to our sovereign lord!'

In London, a far greater pæan was going up to heaven, for that same morning longed-for news of the campaign's outcome had arrived, brought by a fast courier from overseas to the gates of the City. For weeks the Londoners had worried and waited for news, while rumours that the popular young king was dead or captured and his army wiped out had put relatives and friends into a period of premature mourning. Even the Regent, Henry's brother John, Duke of Bedford, had had little in the way of communication since Clarence had arrived home sick from Harfleur. England was racked with apprehension. Masses by the hundred had been offered for the safety of the King and the men.

And now the pursuivant was being conducted to the Guildhall where the newly elected mayor, Alderman Nicholas Wolton (for some indefinable reason nicknamed 'Witless Nick'), received the news of Henry's victory and safe deliverance. Immediately church bells began to peal from parish to parish, St Mary-le-Bow, St Anthony, St Swithin, St Mary Woolchurch, hundreds of chimes all overlaid by the deafening notes of the Jesus Bells of St Paul's, where in the churchyard which served as a public meeting place an enormous mob soon gathered. Henry Beaufort, Bishop of Winchester, addressed the citizens, telling them of the marvellous victory. Queen Joanna, the King's stepmother, organized a procession of thanksgiving. Composed of the new mayor, the aldermen and lords, the burgesses and masters of the guilds of the City, all with their exquisite banners, the company travelled from St Paul's to Westminster, where they knelt before the jewelled shrine of St Edward the Confessor, offering gifts and thanks.

On the following Monday when Parliament opened, Bishop Beaufort delivered a sermon glorifying the King. He commended him for the feat of capturing Harfleur, previously thought impregnable, and for the great triumph at

premierement tu de par le roy
ordene que les gens de la ville
pour ce quilz estoient en tres
grande quantite de mourse
sent aus chams sans entrir
en la ville iusques a ce sien
praise le Roy et tous leurs gens feussent
entre et passe en la ville. Et ainsi fu fait. et
aussi sauoir le Roy sauenir le iour du estant
que nul ne seust si garda le ochin par le chemin
de la grant rue en briant au palais de gris
ne de chanvy ne ne se voug asseut des places
ou ilz estoient mis pour tou lemperier le
roy et le Roy des romniaus paller.

Et de sanc furent aus s
son garde aus louz
nes qui vienent sur
cierent de la grant rue
gardoient et deffendoient
puple de paller. Et le
reioindrent a pie nente des sergens dan
er pasirent le franers de la rue alans h
les clauers du corps du roy leur mie
en leurs pains. leurs espres garmes du
ci cichers. Et pour ce que lemperir a
sauc sauoir an Roy des ce que il vint a
dens que alon vint apare il ne vue
auoir anilz de ses gens pres de lu.

Agincourt. Then, when the Commons were in a state of euphoria, he took the opportunity of stressing that yet more funds were needed to complete in France the campaign that had begun so auspiciously. The idea was accepted without opposition and a substantial grant to the Crown was agreed for this purpose. Also granted to Henry for life was a subsidy on wool, fells and hides, and the wine tax, for which hitherto the King had had to ask yearly, was granted also on this basis, although with the proviso that future monarchs should not regard this as a precedent. Large subsidies 'for the defence of the realm in France' were granted as far in advance as the following autumn.

On 11 November, the Sire de Gaucourt, the Sire d'Estouteville, de Hacqueville and other prominent knights who had pledged their word and been paroled at Harfleur arrived in Calais and paid their ransoms to Henry. A few days later, on 16 November, a fair wind blew up – 'a prosperous gale' – and King, captives and army at last embarked for home. It was a dreadful crossing. The weather was so fierce that two of the ships foundered with all hands and several others were driven in to the Dutch harbour of Zierickzee, lying there until the storm abated. The wretched French captives, most of whom had never set sail in their lives, suffered a nightmare of seasickness, groaning and praying and swearing that their agonies were comparable to those on the day of battle. Their torment was aggravated by the sight of Henry going calmly about his affairs, appearing neither sick nor afraid. However, it appears he was not altogether well; there is a record of medicines being sent earlier from England for the relief of the King's person. But if he were ill he did not show it, and this was a peculiarly courageous trait of his, maintained for the rest of his short life which was terminated by what was probably a virulent amœbic dysentery.

Strapped for their own safety to masts and stanchions, lashed by icy spray, the prisoners endured in misery, knowing

Kings riding in procession.

187

*The French captives, strapped to masts for their own
safety, groaned and prayed.*

that once in London they were to be paraded in triumph, just as they had once envisaged parading Henry through the streets of Paris.

Upon reaching Dover, where howling gales whipped an early snowstorm about their ears, Henry was greeted by the Barons of the Cinque Ports who waded into the icy water to carry him ashore from a longboat. A jubilant mob, almost insane with joy, waited cheering on the shore. He rested a day at Dover and then continued to Canterbury, where he made thank-offerings at the shrine of the martyred St Thomas with its gem-starred canopy, the focal point of which was the Regal of France, known as the finest ruby in the realm. After passing through Rochester he halted at his favourite manor of Eltham, continuing to Blackheath Plain where he was met by the mayor, aldermen and principal guildsmen of the City, dressed in scarlet robes and showing the emblems of their livery companies. Thousands of prominent citizens accompanied them. He came into London on Saturday, 23 November, where a welcome surpassing anything seen before awaited him. And into this he rode, dressed in a plain purple gown, very sober, and unsmiling.

The entry to London took the swelling cavalcade through Southwark where, as in the City across the Thames, bells battered the ear from every church. Except for Henry's exceptionally solemn mien, the occasion was like the triumphant return of a Cæsar. For days since hearing the news of the victory, Londoners had worked ceaselessly to prepare the splendours now awaiting the King. Carpenters, silversmiths, goldsmiths, painters and jewellers had laboured to produce a legendary city within the City.

The first sight that met the eyes of the procession as it crossed London Bridge was that of two giant effigies at each of the Stonegate towers. An enormous sentinel as tall as the towers stood behind a wall of halberds. In his right hand he held an axe and in his left a gold wand from which hung the keys of the City, offered to Henry. This figure was matched by a slightly smaller female one. In a scarlet dress trimmed

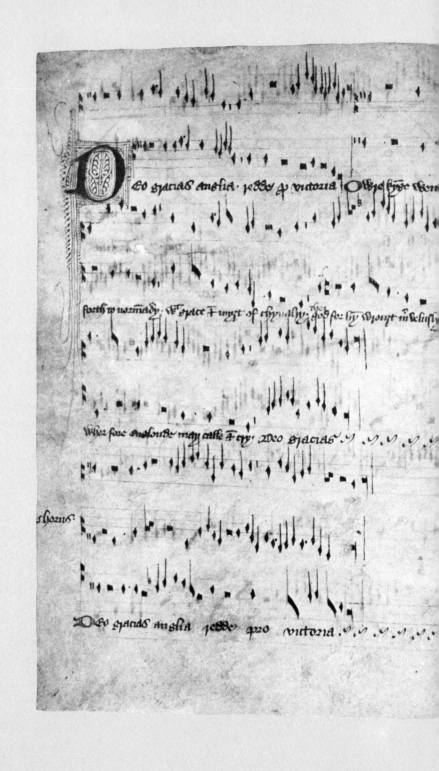

Deo gracias anglia · redde pro victoria · Owr kyng went

forth to normandy · with grace & myзt of chyualry · ther god for hym wrouзt merueluslÿ

Wherfore englonde may calle & cry · Deo gracias ·

chorus ·

Deo gracias anglia · redde pro victoria ·

with jewels and glittering ornaments, she held out a laurel wreath of silver and gold. Between the two effigies hung a scroll painted with the words *Civitas Regis Justiciæ*. Pennons and standards flew in the cold wind on top of the towers. The air was full of music from trumpets, clarions and horns, and as the train rode further into the City more music arose from minstrels on platforms and the turrets of plaster castles, a frenzied spate of high brassy sound changing from street to street, the tail of one tune merging into another and then another. Drums beat loudly, competing with the clatter of the cavalcade and the hectic cheering of the people. 'Hail to the royal City!' said Henry loudly, impressed.

Through the gates the way was lined with temporary columns painted to resemble marble and jasper. On the left, one of these pillars supported a silver-gilt lion bearing the arms of England, and on the right was the figure of Henry's antelope, wearing round its neck a shield with his arms and holding the royal sceptre in its forefoot.

Erected across the street was an enormous bridge crowned with a tapestried crimson pavilion, fringed with hangings in white and jasper. Inside the pavilion was a 20-foot-high representation of St George armed and helmeted, wearing a pearl-studded laurel wreath. Here, hundreds of young boys and pretty girls, their faces painted gold, wearing gold wings and more laurel, sang to an organ accompaniment the new anthem by Lydgate with its six verses.

> Owre King went forth to Normandy,
> With grace and myght of chivalry;
> The God for hym wrought marvelously,
> Wherefore Englonde may call and cry
>   *Deo gratias:*
> *Deo gratias Anglia redde pro victoria.*

Manuscript of John Lydgate's new anthem in celebration of the victory.

The procession of King, lords, dignitaries and clergy with the mortified French noblemen under guard in the middle of the train passed on up Fish Hill to the Cornmarket and then from Leadenhall and Chepeside towards St Paul's. On Cornhill another great crimson pavilion had been set up with its skirts spread wide to reveal the senior citizens 'of venerable hoariness' dressed as the prophets, wearing red and gold turbans and golden mantles. They bowed to the ground, singing Psalm 96 in thanksgiving:

Cantate Domino canticum novum Alleluia!
Quia mirabilis fecit. Alleluia!

before letting fly hundreds of little birds, their feathers tipped with gold paint. They fluttered about the procession, settling for an instant on heads and shoulders. Thousands of cheering people pushed wildly for a better view and were kept in line by men-at-arms. The windows of the houses, leaning so close together that one could shake hands over the street, were crammed with spectators. The roofs were hung with banners, garlands of laurel and streamers. Festoons and tapestries depicting the deeds of past heroes were stretched across the streets which were made narrower still by linen-covered miniature fortresses and castles and by forests of halberds, shields and flags.

When the procession reached St Paul's, more ancient men came out to bow. On their foreheads were written the names of the twelve Apostles, the twelve Kings, Martyrs and Confessors of the realm. They were crowned and held gold sceptres, and chanted Henry's praise. Upon raised velvet platforms were the pick of London's virgins, girdled with gold and laurel and standing motionless. As Henry rode by they softly blew gold leaves from cups of gold on to the King's head. More white-robed girls waited at the steps of the cathedral, playing timbrels, dancing and singing: 'Welcome Henry Fifth, Kynge of England and of Fraunce!' A bevy of small boys in a gilded wooden castle threw from the turrets gold and silver laurel leaves and streamers.

Every citizen was dressed in his or her finest clothes, red or gold seeming to be predominant at this occasion. It is unlikely that there was ever before such a spectacle, or indeed such cause for triumph. By now the stories of courage and carnage had spread – any veteran of Crispin's Day had tales to guarantee him free ale for life – and there was no need for embellishment; the victory's reality was fabulous in itself. Lovers, wives and husbands and children were reunited in the honour of which Henry had spoken in the damp, deathly, fear-filled hours before the battle. The glamour of it all made the people view their young King with unqualified worship. The extravagance of the welcome had strained the City's finances but not one penny was grudged. Gold meant little in the face of this pride and joy.

The men, no longer weary or disillusioned, joined in the riotous celebration with equal joy. They were heroes; they knew their worth and the part they had played to this glorious end. The mud and cold and despairing hunger of the chevauchée seemed a long way off, as did the night before the battle when Henry had comforted them with his calmness, and the smoke and flux and pain of Harfleur seemed like something in another life. The lords too (such as Humphrey of Gloucester, whose wound was healing well) were in high spirits. But Thomas, Duke of Clarence, long recovered from dysentery, was nursing a bitter disappointment. He had missed the entire campaign. In him grew a fierce sense of rivalry with his brother, which would cause him to return one day to France to catch up on past glories, only to jeopardize at the cost of his own life all that had been gained.

In his plain robe, Henry walked forward through the ecstatic crowd in St Paul's Churchyard. He had been pressed to wear the crowned helmet with its battle-scars but had refused. Bareheaded, eyes downcast, he went with eighteen Bishops and his closest attendants into the cathedral where he prostrated himself humbly before the High Altar. Another *Te Deum* was sung, and the Bishops showered Henry with incense. Then the royal party, its progress continually held up by the wild throng that milled forward for a sight of its hero, moved on to Westminster, with Queen Joanna and her priests and knights now accompanying the King. Peal after peal of rejoicing sounded from the Clock House at Westminster and in the great hall sumptuous banquets had been prepared. The mayor and aldermen in their scarlet robes came forward to the dais where the slight, weary, drably clothed figure sat, to present him with tokens of their admiration and affection: a thousand pounds in two gold chalices, each vessel itself worth five hundred pounds.

The progress had lasted five hours. Throughout, Henry remained pensive and humble and whenever men attempted to praise him lavishly he reminded them, clergy, knights and citizens alike, that the great victory was not his but solely God's. Nor was the part played by God's saints forgotten. A synod held the following year ordered the feast of St John of Beverley (7 May) to be kept throughout England, and it continues to be observed in the Roman Catholic diocese of Hexham today.

The banquets prepared for the conqueror's homecoming were doubtless as spectacular as the privation of the campaign had been terrible. At great occasions of this kind three courses were served, each comprising about twelve dishes such as (in the first course): sliced venison in a wheat sauce, meat broth, boar's head, roast haunch of beef, roast swan and piglet, Crustade Lombard (custard with fruit, beef marrow and parsley in a crust); for the second course: jellied soup, capons in almond milk spiced with ginger and herbs, roast pork, heron, pheasant and chicken, roast rabbit and little sweet tarts. The third course might begin with almond soup followed by roast venison, quails and larks, 'payne puff' (egg yolks, marrow, raisins, dates and ginger in a pie), jellies and custards. After each course a 'subtlety' would be brought to the table. These were the masterpieces of the pastrycooks, highly coloured edifices up to four feet high, topped with spun sugar and fashioned in the likeness of saints, castles, battle-scenes, all adorned with sugar animals and heraldic devices, and bearing mottoes in marzipan and icing honouring in French and English the patron of the feast. (Henry's *raison* or motto was UNE SANS PLUS.) Wine was served copiously – the wine of Gascony, the Rhine and Moselle as well as *vin grec* – a heavy sweet import generally made in Calabria. Ypocras (named for Hippocrates) was red or white wine infused with various aromatic ingredients and honey, and was drunk to aid digestion.

In his sober mood it is doubtful whether Henry did justice to this magnificence. More than likely he was thinking again of his unattained dreams. The campaign had been intended to last a year; the achievements of the past four months were, to him, merely the cornerstone on which to build his great empire – the bastion of Christian Europe in the West from where he might at last fulfil his father's dying command and his own ardent desire: to build the walls of Jerusalem against the Infidel.

Now gracious God he save oure Kynge,
His peple, and all his well wyllnge,
Gef him gode lyfe, and gode endynge,
That we with merth mowe savely synge
Deo gratias:
Deo gratias Anglia redde pro victoria.

JOHN LYDGATE: *The Bataille of Agincourt*

King Henry the fifth, too famous to live long!
England ne'er lost a king of so much worth.

SHAKESPEARE: *King Henry VI, Part I,*
Act I, Sc. I

Epilogue It was to be eighteen months before Henry could return to consolidate his gains in France and it was not until 1422 that his dream was realized. While still in England, impatient to begin the new campaign and gathering forces and weapons to this end, he attended to internal affairs, hounding the Lollards, among them the heretic fugitive Sir John Oldcastle, who was later burned in chains. This too Henry saw as all part of the divine plan, an insurance against God forsaking him on his future expeditions to the coveted kingdom. During his preparations for the new assault he wooed and won over the slippery Sigismund of Bohemia. Sigismund, like Henry, was anxious to heal the Great Schism in Europe (at this time there were two Popes, one in Avignon and one in Rome) and by means of both force and diplomatic representations to Rome, they succeeded in this, Sigismund becoming Henry's close ally. Besides this, Henry was in contact with other European rulers likely to aid him in his wars, including King Lewis of the Rhine, and he cast around for princesses among the Dutch and German courts to whom he

Ratification in Parliament of treaty between Henry V and Sigismund of Bohemia.

might, for policy, marry his brothers Bedford and Gloucester.

In spite of the generous subsidies from Parliament, he found his finances grossly straitened, and there was scarcely a jewel of his not in pawn by the time he set sail again from Southampton in July 1417. A vast army accompanied him, for the men of Agincourt had liked the taste of victory. Also they had not, as anticipated, returned enriched for life by ransoms and were glad of a second chance. Fifteen hundred vessels were launched, bearing some 17,000 troops. Armour, great guns, leather pontoons, scaling-ladders and other siege weapons, mallets, spades, picks, gunpowder, longbows and chests of arrows were aboard. Six wing-feathers from every goose in England went to fletch the arrows.

Many of the old commanders again set sail: Gloucester, Huntingdon, Clarence, Salisbury, Cornwall (again with his young son), Talbot, Umfraville, Erpingham, Thomas Beaufort (now made Duke of Exeter) and others who had proved themselves two years earlier. The fleet landed at Touques (where Trouville now stands) and Henry launched his offensive direct into Normandy where, within a day, he captured Bonneville and Auvillars, which surrendered to Salisbury without a blow being struck.

Much to Henry's gratification, France was in possibly a worse state of faction than before. The Dauphin Louis was dead and so was his brother, Jean of Touraine, who, as a partisan of Burgundy, was rumoured to have been murdered by the Armagnacs. Jean sans Peur's star was rising: he appeared to have the whole of northern France on his side. Once again he displayed an equivocal attitude towards the English king, still machinating, scheming, and hoping to find in Henry an ally who would help him crush the rival faction once and for all. For his part, Henry continued to make clear his terms: the realm and throne of France, to which he considered himself returning as a disinherited son, and to seal the bargain, the Princess Catherine in marriage. Her father, Charles of France, was again suffering from bouts of insanity. Her brother Charles, the third Dauphin, seemed unaffected by the perilous vulnerability of his future kingdom and spent most of his time at his hunting lodge near Bourges. Queen Isabeau, wife of the insane king, had now allied herself with Burgundy. Negotiations, so far abortive, were put forward in hopes of settling a marriage portion for Catherine and procuring the best terms with which to satisfy Henry. Promises, threats and arguments flew between the castle at Troyes, where Isabeau was with Jean sans Peur, and Henry's fast-moving encampments, while he confidently came forward and began the campaign which culminated in the ghastly siege of Rouen,

The siege of Rouen.

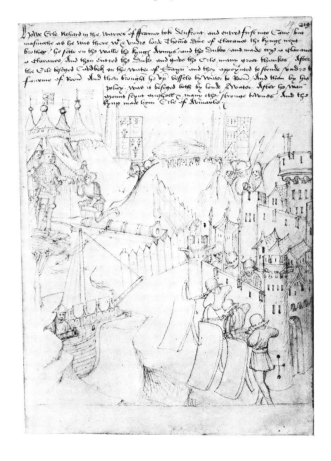

Falaise, birthplace of Henry's mother,

the most brutal of all Henry's campaigns. Lasting for five months, this siege virtually decimated the populace; the people were turned out into the moat between the French and English lines, and babies were born, baptized and died there.

Henry marched first on Caen where, after a gruelling period of attrition, 1800 Frenchmen died hacked to death in the streets by Clarence's men. Young Sir Gilbert Umfraville was left there as Captain and the force moved on, fighting throughout the winter months (something unusual in a medi-

was among the towns recaptured.

eval army), to Falaise, the birthplace of Henry's mother. But his sights were on Paris, totally under the brutal rule of Armagnac and longing to be relieved, if only by Burgundy. By February 1418, Falaise, built on a rock and thought impregnable, was his, and by the end of April, he was the conqueror of all upper Normandy. Paris looked to be within his grasp.

Perhaps his final conquest would not have been so easy but for a diplomatic incident which terminated in murder and brought him an absolute ally. Jean sans Peur had agreed to meet the Dauphin Charles for exploratory talks on the bridge at Montereau. Whether by accident or design, the Duke was hacked to death there. His son Philip of Charolais (the same who had been forbidden the affray at Agincourt) was a placid, pious young man nicknamed 'the Good'. He came to Henry almost immediately, begging for vengeance against the Armagnacs, his father's murderers. The death of Jean sans Peur, Henry was often heard later to say, 'was the hole through which I entered France.'

All this time Henry had striven to bring Europe to his side, wooing the Genoese, the Flemings and the Archbishops of Trèves and Mayence. He had made truces with Brittany and Anjou. City after city meanwhile was falling to his great commanders, Salisbury, Clarence and Warwick: Montivilliers, Lillebonne, Fécamp, Atrepagny, Tancarville, Dieppe, Gournay, Neufchâtel-en-Bray, Eu, Honfleur, Ivry, and La Roche Guyon (taken by Warwick who undermined its foundations). Also Creully, Auvillars, Villars Bocage to the west of Caen, the castle of Alençon, Bayeux, Cherbourg, Louviers and Pont de l'Arche, followed by Lavilleterte and Bouconvillers, Gisors, Meulan, Montjoie and St Germain and Château-Gaillard.

Henry had met the Princess Catherine for the first time on 1 June 1419, when under the ægis of Jean sans Peur she was escorted to his presence in a pavilion outside the West Gate of Meulan opposite the Île Belle on the Seine. He appears to have been pleased with her and later sent a gift of jewellery to the value of 100,000 crowns (stolen in transit by French bandits). His terms for the alliance were, however, unacceptable: he demanded his kingdom still (as inherited from Edward III) upon marriage with the princess, and this included all his own conquests in Normandy, Touraine, Anjou, Maine, Brittany, Flanders, Ponthieu and Montreuil. He named Catherine's dowry at 800,000 crowns (previously agreed upon), but to this Queen Isabeau objected, reminding him that 600,000 crowns were still owing as the dowry taken to England by Catherine's elder sister, Isabella of Valois, when she married

The death of Jean sans Peur on the bridge of Montereau.

Henry went on to besiege and capture more castles.

King Richard II. In reply Henry told the Queen that the ransom for King John, captured by the Black Prince, had never fully been realized. Through mutual intractability the negotiations failed, and Henry went on to besiege and capture more towns and castles, among them Nantes and Pontoise, the stronghold of the Burgundians.

With Philip of Burgundy Henry launched a final assault on the territory he craved. Paris, which had suffered siege and privation under the warring French factions, finally opened to him. With his capture of the town of Tremblay the campaign of vengeance began, while the widowed Duchess of Burgundy fanned the flame, writing in complaint to the Pope and harassing the University of Paris whose patron Jean sans Peur had been. During the following months an almost total capitulation occurred. The Treaty of Troyes was drawn up, the French Parlement acquiesced in Henry's terms and within a short time the Treaty was signed in St Peter's Cathedral at Troyes by the two kings, Philip of Burgundy acting as witness and the Archbishop of Sens officiating. Very soon afterwards Henry and Catherine were married. The Treaty named Henry as King of France on King Charles's demise. Total suzerainty was promised him, together with a substantial dowry for the princess. The following spring, after capturing Sens, Montereau and Melun and entering Paris, he returned with Catherine to England, where a welcome as joyful as that after Agincourt greeted them.

The final desire had been attained and the time was ripe to turn his sights on the crusade to the Holy Land which he saw in his heart as a penance for the act of usurpation by his father Bolingbroke. He had left Thomas, Duke of Clarence in France to counteract any rising by the Armagnacs and the disinherited Dauphin Charles, and was making a progress through the North of England when news arrived to shatter

The wedding of Henry V and Catherine of Valois in the cathedral of Troyes.

his optimism and dislocate his plans. Clarence, still resentful of his unshared glories, had often been heard to say that he could have won the day at Agincourt without the English archers. During a fierce encounter with Dauphinist troops at Baugé in the Loire valley, an incredible foolishness caused Clarence to dispense with the bowmen, and he was killed together with Gilbert Umfraville, Huntingdon and other prominent leaders being captured. Salisbury made a desperate counter-charge into Maine, but Upper Anjou, which had been considered Henry's firmest possession, fell to Armagnac.

Henry returned to France for the last time in June 1421. During a dreadful siege lasting all winter at Meaux, dysentery, the scourge of armies, again decimated his troops. Sir John Cornwall's young son was among those who died, and Henry himself never recovered from the disease. Although mortally ill, he battled on, campaigning with Philip of Burgundy against the Dauphin, and his life ended in the castle of Vincennes, where the last Capetian King had died, on 31 August 1422. Had he survived the death of King Charles a month later, he would truly have become King of England and France. Queen Catherine crossed the Channel to be with him, but the infant son, born in England the previous December and destined to become the tragic, unstable Henry VI, he never saw.

On his deathbed, he requested that the seven penitential psalms be recited, and with his one unfulfilled ambition doubtless in mind declared:

> O Good Lord, thou knowest that, if thy pleasure had been to have suffered me to live my natural age, my firm purpose and intent was, after I had established this realm in France in sure peace, to have gone and visited Jerusalem and to have re-edified the walls thereof, and to have repulsed from it the miscreants, Thine adversaries.

Within the next decade, all that had been accomplished was either lost or slipping away. The warrior-saint, Jeanne d'Arc, had upheld the Dauphin Charles and he was crowned at Rheims in direct contravention of the hard-won Treaty of

The siege of Meaux lasted all winter.

Troyes which was shortly to be annulled by Church and State. The Treaty of Arras, mending the faction between Burgundy and Armagnac, was soon promulgated to restore the inheritance of Valois. The Dukes of Gloucester and Bedford struggled on for a while, managing eventually to retain only Calais and a few minor English holdings. At Chinon, Jeanne had infected the apathetic young Dauphin with her blazing zeal and, appointing the new Duke of Alençon as her commander, she relieved the town of Orléans (which the Earl of Salisbury had earlier died capturing) and then threw her forces on Tourelles, St Loup, Patay, Auxerre, Châlons and Rheims. Paris declared her allegiance to Charles VII and his descendants. The betrayal of Jeanne by Charles is a shameful fact, but before her burning at the hands of Bedford and Warwick, her mystic purpose had been irrevocably fulfilled. The glory of Agincourt and the splendour of Crispin's Day had become a tawdry myth.

The great Henry lay lapped in stone under a carved canopy in St Edward's Chapel, Westminster, surmounted by a silver effigy, his achievements, sword, and broken battle-helm displayed as tokens of his courage and his brief hour of fame. The bones had been boiled from his pathetic wasted body and carried home in a leisurely mourning procession from Vincennes to Abbeville, Hesdin, Montreuil, Boulogne, to Calais and Dover. A complete death-mask of head and face and body had been moulded in boiled leather and fixed on top of the bier. This mask was crowned with an imperial diadem of gold and rubies and clothed in a purple robe trimmed with ermine. In the effigy's right hand was placed a sceptre and in the left an orb. The elaborate H-shaped chantry chapel where Henry still lies was not completed for some years, but each year on Crispin's Day the morning communion service is held here as a token of remembrance. The widowed Queen

The altar in Henry V's elaborate H-shaped chantry chapel in Westminster Abbey.

Henry V on his charger. A detail from his
chantry chapel.

Catherine commissioned her husband's silver effigy on the
tomb before forming a liaison with the young esquire Owen
ap Meredyth ap Tydier, the offspring of which were to found
the Tudor dynasty.

Never again would the great Harry of England ride forth
in conquest. Never again would France bow to England, or

its plains and battlements echo with English cries of triumph. It is as well that he knew nothing of the ultimate recession and the irreversible loss of dominions for which he had fought so ardently as his right. Today we see Henry V as an extraordinary man and monarch, dedicated and ruthless, although certainly no more ruthless than his contemporaries. We see his astonishing energy, his supernormal powers of inspiring leadership in a disheartened, sickly force facing insuperable odds. We see him devoured by a dream and a cause. We see him capable of infecting others with his zeal and dedication. We see his 'little touch of Harry in the night'.

Fortune naturally had a hand in Crispin's Day: the total disunity and disorganization of his adversaries, the favourable terrain and the mobility of the English forces, and moreover the sagacity of his commanders – Erpingham, Huntingdon, Camoys, York, Umfraville and the others – all this weighed heavily in his favour. Yet the outcome of the battle cannot be dismissed as a lucky chance. The following campaigns, which made Henry supreme in conquest if only for a season, confirm that here was a man of valour seldom seen before or since.

The word 'Agincourt' still has glamour while, strangely, the subsequent unhappy events, the loss of the French dominions, are forgotten. The day is immortalized in the words of Shakespeare, Drayton, Elmham and Lydgate: the echo of the song which greeted the victor on that day of gold and flowers so long ago.

> Upon Saint Crispin's Day
> Fought was this noble fray
> Which fame did not delay
> To England to carry.
> O when shall English men
> With such acts fill a pen?
> Or England breed again
> Such a King Harry?

Bibliography

Belleval, René de: *La Grande Guerre*. 1862

Burne, A. H.: *The Agincourt War – A Military History of the latter part of the Hundred Years' War from 1369 to 1453*. London, 1956

Butler's *Lives of the Saints*, ed. H. J. Thurston, SJ and Donald Attwater. London, 1956

Churchill, Winston S.: *History of the English Speaking Peoples*. Vol. I: *The Birth of Britain*. London, 1956

Earle, Peter: *The Life and Times of Henry V*. London, 1972

Fowler, Kenneth: *The Age of Plantagenet and Valois*. London, 1967

Gaunt, William: *Oxford*. London, 1965

Hibbert, Christopher: *Agincourt*. London, 1964

Jacob, E. F.: *Henry V and the Invasion of France*. London, 1947; *The Fifteenth Century (1399–1485)*. London, 1961

Labarge, Margaret Wade: *Henry V, The Cautious Conqueror*. London, 1975

Lindsay, Philip: *King Henry V*. London, 1934

Nicolas, Sir Harris: *History of the Battle of Agincourt*. 1832

Reade, Compton (ed.): *Memorials of Old Herefordshire*. London, 1904

Thomas Rymer's *Foedera, Conventiones, Litterae et cujuscunque generis Acta Publica inter Reges Angliae* (1709). Printed in full in Nicolas, q.v.

Sass, Lorna: *To the King's Taste*. New York, 1975

Thomas de Elmham (attr.): *Vita et Gesta Henrici Quinti Anglorum Regis*. (ed. Thomas Hearne, 1727). Coll. Arms, Arundel MS.

Tito Livio Foro: (Tito Livio of Forli): *Juliensis Vita Henrici Quinti* (ed. Thomas Hearne, 1716). Cambridge University, Corpus Christi Ms. N. 31

Uden, Grant: *A Dictionary of Chivalry*. London, 1967

Illustrations Acknowledgements

78   PRO E 101/51.

80-1 Bildarchiv der Österreichischen
      Nationalbibliothek, Cod. 2617
      f.19.

83   BN MS lat. 919 f.96.

85   BN MS fr. 836, t.II, f.1.

87   Koninklijk Museum voor Schone
      Kunsten, Antwerp.

89   Musée Jacquemart-André, Paris,
      Heures du Maréchal de Boucicaut
      f.26^V, Photo: Giraudon.

91   BN MS lat. 18014 f.288^V.

93   BL MS Cotton Julius E IV art. 6
      f.12.

95   BL MS Harley 289 f.211^V.

97   BN MS Arsenal 5189 f.152^V.

100   BL MS Royal 20 cvii f.78^V.

101   BL Add. MS 27697 f.194^V.

106   BL MS Royal 14 E IV f.57.

108   BN MS fr. 2663 f.164.

109   By courtesy of the Dean and Chap-
      ter of Westminster.

110   BN MS fr. 22547 f. 76.

113 BL MS Harley 326 f.90.

117   Bibliothèque Royale Albert Ier,
      Brussels, MS 9242 f.184.

119   (above) BL MS Nero E II (2) f.166;
      (below) BL MS Yates Thomson 33
      f.74.

120-1 BL MS Royal 20 cvii f.136^V.

125 BL MS Cotton Julius E IV art. 6
      f.8^V.

128 BN MS 2675 f.cl.

131   BL MS Royal 20 cvii f.27^V.

134   BL MS Royal 20 cvii f.13^V.

135   BL MS Royal 20 cvii f.137.

136   Musée Jacquemart-André, Paris,
      Heures du Maréchal de Boucicaut
      f.38^V, Photo: Giraudon.

139   BL MS Cotton Julius E IV art. 6
      f.14.

143   BN MS 2691 f.197.

147   BN MS lat. 6067 f.85^V.

152   By courtesy of the Dean and Chap-
      ter of Westminster.

157   BL MS Cotton Julius E IV art. 6
      f.4.

161   BL MS Harley 4431 f.110.

164-5 Lambeth Palace Library, *St Albans
      Chronicle*.

168 BN MS 5041 f.11.

172-3 BN MS fr. 2691 f.38.

176 Musée Condé, Chantilly, *Les Treès
      Riches Heures du Duc de Berry*,
      Photo: Giraudon.

179   BL MS Cotton Julius E IV art. 6
      f.27.

182   BL MS Royal 16 F2 f.73.

186   BN MS 6465 f.44^V.

188   BL MS Cotton Julius E IV art. 6
      f.25.

190   Bodleian Library, Oxford, MS
      Bodley 175A, MS Arch Seld B26
      f.17^V.

196   PRO E 30 391.

199   BL MS Cotton Julius EIV art. 6
      f.19^V.

201   BL MS Yates Thomson 33 f.89.

203   BN MS Arsenal 5084 f.1.

204-5 BL MS Royal 14 E IV f.59^V.

207   BL MS Cotton Julius E IV art. 6
      f.22.

209   BL MS Royal 20 cvii f.134.

211 & By courtesy of the Dean and Chap-
213   ter of Westminster.

Index

(Figures in *italic* type refer to illustrations)

219